Helion & Company Limited
Unit 8 Amherst Business Centre
Budbrooke Road
Warwick
CV34 5WE
England
Tel. 01926 499 619
Email: info@helion.co.uk
Website: www.helion.co.uk
Twitter: @helionbooks
Visit our blog http://blog.helion.co.uk/

Designed & typeset by Farr out Publications, Wokingham, Berkshire
Cover design by Paul Hewitt, Battlefield Design (www.battlefield-design.co.uk)

Printed for Helion & Co by Henry Ling Ltd., Dorchester, Dorset

ISBN 978-1-911628-63-7

British Library Cataloguing-in-Publication Data
A catalogue record for this book is available from the British Library

We always welcome receiving book proposals from prospective authors.

Contents

Note: In order to simplify the use of this book, all names, locations and geographic designations are as provided in *The Times World Atlas*, or other traditionally accepted major sources of reference, as of the time of described events. Correspondingly, the term 'Congo' designates the area of the former Belgian colony of the Congo Free State, granted independence as the Democratic Republic of the Congo in June 1960 and in use until 1971 when the country was renamed Republic of Zaire, which, in turn, reverted to Democratic Republic of the Congo in 1997, and which remains in use today. As such, Congo is not to be mistaken for the former French colony of Middle Congo (Moyen Congo), officially named the Republic of the Congo on its independence in August 1960, also known as Congo-Brazzaville.

Abbreviations

ANC	*Armée Nationale Congolaise* (Congolese National Army)
BiAF	Biafran Air Force
BOFF	Biafran Organisation of Freedom Fighters
CO	commanding officer
COIN	counter insurgency
DRC	Democratic Republic of the Congo (also 'Congo-Kinshasa')
FN/FAL	Fabrique Nationale (Herstal)/Fusil Automatique Léger (light automatic rifle of Belgian origin)
GBP	British Pounds Sterling
GOC	general officer commanding
HQ	headquarters
Il	Ilyushin (the Soviet aircraft design bureau led by Sergey Vladimirovich Ilyushin, also known as OKB-39)
MiG	Mikoyan i Gurevich (the Soviet aircraft design bureau led by Artyom Ivanovich Mikoyan and Mikhail Iosifovich Gurevich, also known as OKB-155 or MMZ 'Zenit')
MWLA	Mid-West Liberation Army
NAF	Nigerian Air Force
NYT	New York Times
OAU	Organisation of African Unity
RAP	Department of Research and Production (Biafran authority)
RSM	Regimental Sergeant-Major
STF	Special Task Force (Biafran Army)

Dedication

This book is dedicated to the late Romano Cagnoni and all the other photographers and journalists who highlighted the plight of Biafran civilians during the Nigerian Civil War.

Acknowledgments

My thanks go to Peter Abbott, the late Romano Cagnoni, John De St Jorre, David Spencer, Al J Venter and Paul.V.Walsh.

Introduction

The Nigerian Civil War, which lasted from May 1967 until January 1970, was one of the most destructive conflicts in 20th century African history. Although it was not Africa's first modern war it was certainly the first African conflict to get substantial media attention. It was the scale of the suffering, especially of the starving civilian population which meant that it competed for press coverage with the Vietnam War. It was the suffering and mass starvation of civilians, and especially the children of Eastern Nigeria, that grabbed the headlines between 1968 and 1970. Beginning only seven years after the huge country of Nigeria had gained independence from the British Empire it was to cause millions of deaths. Described at first in the news as a rebellion by a 'crazy' maverick colonel in a faraway African country it soon began gaining attention for other reasons. Anyone who was old enough to remember the war will recall the images of starving children in the media and because of the related coverage it was the first time that malnutrition had made headlines in the West. At times its tragedies even eclipsed the nightly news reports from Vietnam that dominated TV-screens. Another feature of the media coverage was the continued stubborn resistance of the Biafran people and their armed forces. They often fought with fanatical bravery with rifles against the tanks, artillery and jets of the Nigerian Armed Forces. Although the war was never the simple 'David versus Goliath' conflict that it was frequently portrayed as, it was an uneven and a deadly contest. Many foreign commentators and journalists became obsessed with explaining why and how Biafra survived for 30 months: how did Biafra's 'ramshackle' army, navy and its air force continue to resist the Nigerians for so long? Indeed, the Biafrans managed to resist an army that during the war grew into the largest such in Sub-Saharan Africa: when the war began the 9,000 strong Nigerian Army was faced by a Biafran army of about 3,000 men. As the federal Nigerian Army expanded to a strength of about 120,000, the Biafran Army never managed to recruit more than 40,000 personnel.

When the large and populous West African state of Nigeria achieved independence from Great Britain in October 1960, the future for the country looked bright. It was relatively well-prepared for independence, had a comparatively well-developed infrastructure, and a relatively mature political system – especially in comparison to the Democratic Republic of the Congo (DRC), released into independence by Belgium in 1960. That said, Nigeria was still troubled by deep underlying tribal tensions. The 25 million people living in the country at the time were split into about 250 tribal groups, of which four formed 'nations': the Yoruba in the west, the Hausa and Fulani in the north, and the Ibos in the south-east. As usual in the British imperial possessions, some groups were seen as 'more cooperative' than the others: the Ibo tribe was considered 'most industrious', and often performed similar roles to those of the Sikhs in imperial India before 1947. Large numbers of the Ibo thus moved to other regions of the country, were employed in the administration and diverse civil services, or ran businesses. By 1966 there were 1,300,000 'easterners' living and working in the north of the country with another 500,000 living in the west. As the Ibos tended to take the most desirable jobs a level of resentment grew amongst the Hausa, Yoruba and other tribes.

Dominated by loyalties to the tribe, Nigerian politics was divided correspondingly: the first post-independence elections were held in December 1964 and won by a party dominated by the northerners. The result was challenged by the westerners and easterners alike, causing rifts along both geographical and tribal lines. The resulting political crisis grew further in the aftermath of – supposedly – 'rigged' elections held in the west of Nigeria in October 1965. Accusations of political irregularities and corruption grew with the different regions accusing the others of jeopardising democracy by their behaviour.

Although including a number of idealistic young officers, the Nigerian armed forces of the early 1960s were mostly drafted according to tribal association. Many of the politically-minded officers monitored the growing corruption of the politicians with dismay. They soon began plotting coups d'état, aiming to install military governments instead. Indeed, announcing that the 'corrupt government must be destroyed', on 15 January 1966, mutinous troops led by Chukwuma Kaduna Nzeogwu and Emmanuel Ifeajuna launched the first *putsch*. It was a crude, brutal operation that shocked the world with the summary execution of at least 22 people – including the Prime Minister of Nigeria, the leaders of the northern and western regions, and several top military officers along with their wives. In the ensuing chaos, the young officers were skilfully outmanoeuvred by the shrewd Major-General Johnson Aguiyi-Ironsi, Chief-of-Staff of the Army, who formed a military government just a day later. Ironsi, an Ibo, stabilised the situation, but his rule was to be short-lived. Unprepared to accept the new strongman due to his tribal background, on 29 July a group of officers from the north staged a new, equally brutal coup: Ironsi and a number of his deputies were taken into the bush, tortured for information and then summarily executed. This coup was followed by the arrest and execution of all Ibo officers: the lucky ones were shot on the spot, while the less fortunate had their throats cut. One was tied to a cross and beaten to death, while Major Don Okafor – a member of the plot from January 1966 – was buried alive. The few that survived were humiliated through being forced to consume their own urine and faeces. By the time the frenzy was over, at least 41 Ibo officers of the army, two from the air force, and 194 soldiers of eastern origin were killed, and 23 other easterners from diverse tribes were missing: 154 of these were Ibo. Anyone who was still around was desperately trying to escape to the east.

In the aftermath of the coup, the dormant grievances against the Ibo grew – especially in the north. Indeed, the northern hatred for the Ibos and other easterners reached a fever pitch. During September and October anti-Ibo riots resulted in the horrific deaths of about 30,000 easterners. The survivors fled east, often missing limbs, and spreading stories of outrages and hysteria. Eventually, over 600,000 easterners found refugee under protection of the military governor of the region, Colonel Chukwuemeka Odumegwu Ojukwu.

Himself an Ibo, Ojukwu was 34-years-old, and not only a military commander but also an ambitious politician. Before long, he began demanding wider autonomy for the east and reassurances about the safety of easterners, and then – angered by the treatment of his fellow easterners – began acting against all foreigners. He seized the Federal Government assets and began to expel northerners, claiming this was for their own protection. The Colonel also began to lobby his fellow easterners to back the secession of the region and create an independent state – an outlook that appeared promising because the east had a well-educated population of seven million and substantial oil reserves.

Back in Lagos, the newly-installed junta led by 32-year-old Lieutenant-General Jack Gowon, appealed to Ojukwu. A member of the minority Tiy tribe, Gowon was widely regarded as a 'compromise leader' who could balance the rivalries between diverse parts of the country. Moreover, he suspected that Ojukwu was about to secede the east and thus repeatedly warned the governor to abandon any related plans. When this showed no results, several attempts were launched in late 1966 to keep Nigeria intact through setting up military councils. The last of these was held in January 1967 on neutral ground at Aburi in Ghana: Ojukwu attended but had meanwhile made his decision, and was actively plotting secession. Thus no settlement was found. Indeed, over the following months he accused Gowon of breaking promises and before long it was obvious that the leader of the easterners was going as far as to purchase arms to bolster his military capabilities and defend the new state once it emerged. Gowon reacted by declaring the formation of the Nigerian Federation, consisting of 12 states, which divided the east into three. The die was cast: knowing he would remain in the position of a governor, but have his powers limited to just one of the three newly-declared states, Ojukwu was forced to act. On 31 May 1967, he formally declared the secession of the east as a new state named The Republic of Biafra (named after the Bight of Biafra, a coastal channel).

Adamant, Gowon reacted by announcing that Biafra's succession would not be taken lying down – even if that meant a damaging civil war.

Preparing for Secession

The Biafran preparations for secession can be traced back to August 1966, as the last non-eastern military personnel left Enugu. Without the presence of troops who were against secession to bother them, the pro-secession officials and army officers could now openly prepare for the expected war. The grand total of eastern soldiers left at Enugu Barracks was down to 240 men and these were nearly all technicians and support troops. Even by the most optimistic prediction this was not enough to build a viable armed force, but it was a start. Over the next few months, as secret arms shipments began to arrive in Enugu, it was decided to raise two battalions of troops. Before long, the Biafrans had enough rifles, and a few machineguns, to equip small units: what they lacked was artillery, armoured vehicles and other heavy weaponry.

As the tension between the newly declared state of Biafra and the rest of the country built up after the 31 May secession, Ojukwu exuded an air of quiet confidence: indeed, during the short period between secession and the outbreak of the war, his calmness impressed many visiting journalists. However, it failed to convince his fellow officers, all – reasonably – worried about their future. Curiously, while overly interested in reassuring his companions, Ojukwu did pay attention to reassuring the civilian leaders. In a famous propaganda stunt he took high-ranking civilians to the base of the newly-established 1st Battalion's firing range outside Enugu, and demonstrated to them the newly-acquired automatic rifles and machineguns.[1] On another occasion a visiting Yoroba Chief was treated to an aerial display by two French made Alouette III helicopters which were painted in the Biafran colours. With such demonstrations Ojukwu hoped to convince not only his enemies in Lagos but also some of his own people of the Biafran armed forces' capabilities. In one of his many pre-war boasts, Ojukwu told the press in no uncertain terms about his confidence in the east's ability to defend itself saying:

> I am proud and my officers are proud that here in the east, we possess the biggest army in Africa. I am no longer speaking as an underdog; I am speaking from a position of power. It is not my intention to unleash destruction, which my army can unleash. It is not my intention to fight unless I am attacked: if I am attacked, I will take good care of the aggressor![2]

Ojukwu's overconfidence was also exemplified by the much-quoted fact that he expected the war to last three months. Some of his officers were even more deluded and thought that Ojukwu was being pessimistic and that it should be won in two weeks!

However, generally speaking, Biafran officers did not share their leader's confidence and wondered how they could defend the new state with no rifles. They were particularly worried how they and their men were to defend their frontiers without the promised arms. Their worries were not allayed by Ojukwu who seldom met with his commanders in the weeks after Biafra's secession. When they did get to ask him about when the promised arms were going to arrive he blithely answered, 'They are in the pipeline'.

Chapter 1
Establishment of the Biafran Armed Forces

The Biafran Army was established in May 1967 around a core of a few hundred officers and men organised into a single battalion. When new arms arrived in Biafra, later the same month, two additional units came into being: the 9th and the 14th Battalions. From that moment onwards, the size and composition of the army was going to remain limited by the number of rifles and other arms it could acquire.

Command Structure

Throughout the Nigerian Civil War, Colonel Ojukwu was the undisputed military leader of the Biafran Armed Forces; he was the Commander-in-Chief, supported by a small staff made up of his aide-de-camp, a military advisor, a liaison officer and a personal assistant. Further down the hierarchy was the Chief-of Staff: his headquarters (HQ) was made up of five sections (or branches):

- General Staff (G Branch)
- Adjutant General's Staff (A Branch)
- Quarter Master Branch (Q Branch)
- Defence Operations Branch, and
- Camp Commands Branch.

Below the Chief of Staff in the chain of command was the General Officer Commanding (GOC) at Army Headquarters with its leader responsible for the day-to-day operations of the Biafran Army. He was supposed to work in close co-operation with the Commanders of the Air Force and the Navy. Nominally, the GOC was to report to the Chief of Staff; but, in reality, he had direct access to the Commander-in-Chief. Next in the order of command were officers commanding divisions, brigades, battalions and their support arms and service units. The fluid situation in the organisation of every Biafran division and brigade meant that the command structure at this level was often ignored. By 1968 there were two army HQs:

- Main HQ at Agwu Leadership Camp, and
- Tactical HQ, originally situated in Enugu.

Major Units

By the time the fighting began in earnest in July 1967, the Biafran Army had seven poorly armed battalions: three of these were grouped into the 51st Brigade that defended the university town of Nsukku in the north; the 11th protected the central sector with the capital Enugu; while most of the remaining units were concentrated in the Port Harcourt area, protected by the 52nd Brigade. For the rest of 1967, the army experienced no further expansion except for the establishment of the 1,000-strong 101st Division with the purpose of launching the Mid-West invasion of August: this was disbanded after the failure of the Mid-West operation, and its survivors were used to form three new battalions for the defence of Onitsha. Additional divisions were established in January 1968: the second of these – the 12th Division – originally including the 55th and 56th Brigades, but because the 55th was too far away from its headquarters, it was replaced by the 58th Brigade. Later on, the 12th Division was reinforced by the addition of the 71st Brigade, nominally becoming the biggest formation of this size. After the 13th Division was established in 1968, two other brigades that proved themselves in combat were expanded to the same status. Finally, the Special Task Force (STF) was formed to fight in the Arochukwu sector after the fall of Umhuahia in June 1969: like the other large formations, it had a rather loose organisation was only intended to operate as a divisional-level command for a specific period of fighting.

The Biafran Army also included a number of independent Infantry Brigades, including the 53rd, 57th, 61st, 62nd, 64th, 65th, 66th, 69th and 73rd. Although the organisation of these units was to say the least 'fluid' they generally were made up of 2 battalions. Some

Table 1: Major Units of the Biafran Army, 1967-1970

Designation	Elements	Notes
51st Brigade	3 battalions	est. Jul 1967; defending Nsukku
11th Brigade	3 battalions	est. Aug 1967; defending Enugu
101st Division		est. Jul 1967; 1,000-strong; disbanded Sep 1967
11th Division	54th Brigade 57th Brigade	est. Jan 1968
12th Division	55th then 58th Brigade 56th Brigade 71st Brigade	est. Jan 1968
13th Division	51st Brigade 55th Brigade	est. Jan 1968; 2,000-strong; re-designated 15th Division
4th Commando Brigade		expanded into division in 1968
S Brigade		expanded into division in 1968
14th Division	52nd Brigade 60th Brigade	est. 1968
Special Task Force		est. Jun 1969 in Arochukwu sector
Republic of Benin Brigade		est. 1969

Colonel Chukwuemeka Ojukwu, the former Eastern State Military Governor and now leader of secessionist Biafra sits smoking at his Enugu Headquarters in May 1967. Ojukwu issued a number of bombastic statements before the fighting began in an attempt to impress the Federal Government. His claims of large stockpiles of armaments and his announcement that his people were ready to, "Commit mass suicide" was meant to intimidate the enemy. Unfortunately for Ojukwu he was faced by an equally determined foe, Major-General Yakubu Gowon. (Author's Collection)

Civilian volunteers undergo training for the Biafran Militia armed mainly with crudely carved wooden rifles. The marching column is led by a woman wearing the 'Be Vigilant' t-shirt sold to volunteers by street market dealers. Just like the British Local Defence Volunteers of 1940 these enthusiastic men and women try to look as military as possible. Two of the volunteers have managed to acquire double barrelled shotguns which were the most lethal weapons available in the summer of 1967. (Author's Collection)

brigades were formed on an ad-hoc basis for particular operations and their constituent battalions regularly changed. According to Biafran Army sources the acquisition of a few hundred rifles would mean the raising of other ad-hoc battalions. The average Biafran Army battalion was made up of between 400 and 600 men who were armed on average with 2-300 bolt-action Mauser or Lee-Enfield rifles, 10 – 15 vz. 58 assault rifles and about 30 West German H&K G3 assault rifles (or its Spanish CETME equivalent). The CETME's were usually reserved for the 'shock' platoon of every battalion which received the best arms and equipment. The number of machineguns was limited to 2-3 light machineguns and one heavy machinegun per battalion and they were of very different types (see below). Mortars were usually concentrated at brigade level and deployed only on neuralgic spots. Ammunition was also held at brigade level and was allocated to smaller units on a day by day basis. Support units in the battalion were made up of a signal platoon with at most a couple of shortwave radios. There was also an engineer unit which could have between 30 and 50 men with responsibility for the construction of fortifications and digging trenches, and were often also tasked with operating home-made/do-it-yourself weaponry.

The 'S' Brigade: 'Strike' Division

During the demoralising defeats of 1967, Ojukwu surrounded himself with a number of trusted soldiers and policemen. Every member of this entourage was ready to protect the leader with his life, especially against any possible conspiracies by army officers. One of the Biafran leader's bodyguards, Regimental Sergeant-Major Williams was seen as the inspiration for the formation of a 'Praetorian

Mixed male and female militia march through the streets of Enugu in the early days of the war with Nigeria. The severe shortage of rifles meant that the Militia had to make do with wooden rifles for the time being. Later some were issued with machetes and were sent against the Federal Army advancing on the Biafran capital. Thankfully the thousands of machete armed volunteers facing reality broke up and returned to their own lines before too many were killed by Nigerian machineguns. (Author's Collection)

A local militia unit is inspected by the District Officer in the early stages of the Civil War in the summer of 1967. The organisation of Militia and Civil Defenders during the war was done on a local basis and any arms had to be sourced locally. Like the British Home Guard of 1940 the Biafran Home Guard in 1967 would have been lucky to have a few shotguns per unit. Others were 'armed' with wooden rifles carved usually by the men and women themselves or with crudely made machetes. (Author's Collection)

Guard', designed to protect Ojukwu. Williams had proved his bravery in the confused fighting in the north and his loyalty to Ojukwu was unquestioned. What Ojukwu really wanted was a unit full of men like Williams and a search began for officers and soldiers untainted by the army's failures and conspiracies of 1967.

Most of those drafted for this task came from amongst the ranks of the Port Harcourt Militia, were students, or mere schoolboys. The primary criteria for their selection was total loyalty to Ojukwu (indeed, military experience was considered secondary). Without exception, they all proved very enthusiastic, even if not well-trained. Eventually, the 400 troops of the 'S' Brigade included only the odd policemen and a few veteran soldiers displaced by the war. With the exception of two men – both personally selected by Ojukwu – officers that had served in the pre-1967 Nigerian Army were not allowed to join this unit: the two exceptions were Lieutenant-Colonel Onwuatuegwu and Major Frank Obioha, who were widely considered the best officers of the entire Biafran Army.

While organised into three battalions and receiving its own insignia (a red lightning flash on a black background), the 'S'

Two Militia volunteers stand guard in front of the recruiting office set up to sign up the thousands of men and women who came forward after May 1967. A uniform of sorts was issued to a few Militiamen with grey shirts featuring a large letter 'M' on the left shoulder. The man on the left is armed with a crude dane gun which has the firing mechanism of a 19th century musket. (Author's Collection)

Civil Defenders armed with crudely made machetes look menacingly at the camera from the roadblock they are manning. The paranoia in Biafra during the war meant that men and boys like these could hand out summary justice to anyone they thought was a possible spy. Soldiers, especially officers, were often the victims of these 'upholders' of justice if suspected of desertion or other military crimes, usually without any evidence. (Author's Collection)

Brigade was not considered a combat unit. All of its officers, from the commander – Colonel Onwuategwu – and its battalion commanders – Majors Archibong and Atumaka – were granted easy access to Ojukwu and were allowed to visit State House whenever they wanted. Officers of the 'S' Brigade were also given preferential treatment when it came to the issue of uniforms, arms and equipment. This favouritism naturally caused a great deal of bad feeling between members of the unit and the rest of the army.

Two Civil Defenders travel home after a day looking for 'saboteurs' around their village in the summer of 1967. Men like these spent their days stopping cars and 'combing' the surrounding rainforest looking for anyone suspicious. The man on the left is one of the fortunate ones who has acquired a firearm even if it is a dane gun modelled on an early 19th century musket. (Author's Collection)

In early 1968, Onwuategwu was approached by a couple of men who wanted to organise a special unit within the 'S' Brigade. Their plan was to establish an elite commando unit, members of which were to receive additional training. Onwuategwu authorised this plan under the condition that the commando element remain limited to about 50 men. Their special regiment included lectures in construction and deployment of such home-made weaponry as Molotov cocktails, armament manufactured by the Department of Research and Production (RAP), diverse rockets, and the famed Ogbunigwe (see below for details). The resulting 'Rangers Regiment' consisted of hand-picked junior officers and non-commissioned officers (NCOs) of the 'S' Brigade.

For the rest of the 'S' Brigade, the easy life came to an end with the fall of the Biafran capital of Enugu. Before long, they found themselves fighting alongside their army comrades, already resentful for all the favouritism shown to the unit. However, most bad feelings faded away during the following months, as its troops proved their mettle in combat. Indeed, following positive experiences, permission was granted to expand the Rangers Regiment to 200, usually deployed in detachments 40-50 strong for commando operations behind enemy lines, or as experts for RAP weapons.

As the 'S' Brigade continued to prove itself during the summer of 1968 it was decided to expand it into a division. Necessary arms were acquired from the 4th Commando Brigade after this suffered extensive losses in the battles for Aba and Onitsha. Brought to a total of about 1,200 troops, and still commanded by Colonel Onwuategwu, the 'S' Division was organised into three brigades: the original 'S' Brigade, now under the command of Major Atumaka, plus the 67th (Major Okoi) and 68th (Major Archibong, one of several Biafran officers that earned himself the reputation of being 'bullet proof', regardless how often he put himself in dangerous situations).[1]

During the rest of 1968 and into 1969 the division earned the respect of the rest of the Biafran Army: far from being seen as 'prima donnas', its officers were now highly regarded. While still under the command of Colonel Onwuategwu, the division was then deployed against the Nigerian 16th Brigade besieged in Owerri but suffered heavy casualties. Ojukwu then intervened and split the division into two, assigning the other half to Colonel Joe Achuzia

Civil Defenders patrol around their village in the early days of the war armed with nothing more lethal than a tree branch. Men like this would soon be recruited into the Biafran Army leaving their role to be performed by older men and boys. (Author's Collection)

During early fighting in the Civil War in the Northern region of the breakaway state of Biafra, prisoners are roughly moved to military prison. Surprisingly the ones with all the 'spit and polish' are the Biafran soldiers while their Nigerian prisoners are less well turned out. According to the original caption the prisoners may well be Chadian immigrants to Nigeria who were tempted to join the Federal Army for the relatively high pay. (Author's Collection)

– widely perceived as an amateur upstart, and certainly no friend of Onwuategwu. Achuzia led his men towards Owerri and got to within a kilometre of the town but was forced to withdraw after suffering heavy casualties in pointless frontal assaults. The two rival commanders and their retinues had a confrontation which ended with both of them drawing their pistols. Ojukwu then intervened for a second time and came down on the side of Achuzia: only another week of costly failures convinced him to re-unite the 'S' Division under Onwuategwu again.

The Directorates

When the Biafran Army came into being in May 1967, the few regular soldiers available were assigned to the newly raised infantry battalions. Any army needs the vital support branches which take care of supplying the combat units with food, munitions, fuel and clothing. Because of the extreme circumstances faced by Biafra in 1967, it was decided to harness the enthusiasm of the civilian population to run these support branches. The decision to de-militarise the administrative and support services of the army was not really a good idea and the Biafrans had little choice but to establish directorates responsible for acquiring food, fuel, transport and clothing for the army. Civil servants were appointed to fill the roles and in some cases they did a reasonable job. However, in many cases the directorates and their overbearing red tape simply complicated and hampered the Biafran war effort. Bureaucracy went into overdrive, and the civil servants and enthusiastic amateurs who ran the directorates often got in the way of the armed forces' efforts.

Food for the Army

Few if any of the staff of the directorates of the Biafran armed forces had military experience or knew how to appreciate the needs of an army deployed in the field. Perhaps the worst of all was the Food Directorate, where the lack of efficiency and necessary preparations became glaringly obvious right from the start. As a result, troops frequently went into the battle literally hungry. The Food Directorate reacted by establishing cookhouses behind the frontlines, where the food was prepared and then transported to the frontline units. The lucky ones were then provided with true 'packed lunches'. However, as food became scarcer, this system began falling apart and the entire supply chain became chaotic – even more so because the lack of communication between military and civilian officials meant that most of the military operations had to be scheduled to coincide with food deliveries, instead of the other way around. Even when food was cooked at the right time transport difficulties could cause a breakdown in the delivery of food. The fact that the cookhouses were operated by civilians meant that during Federal offensives they had to be re-deployed to safer locations: in other words, just when the soldiers needed their food the most, there was usually a breakdown in supply and the troops went hungry.

The Food Directorate was also responsible for supplying units with cigarettes and drinks. For the reasons described above, this meant that the troops usually fought without such 'luxuries'. Army officers soon angrily demanded that Ojukwu give them the responsibility and means to feed their own men. To their despair, he refused to get rid of the civilians running the food supply system, mainly because of his lack of trust in the army. The excuse was used was that the more powerful officers would take all the available food for their units and leave the others hungry. Meanwhile the Chairman of the Directorate made an insulting suggestion that his staff be given military ranks and uniforms without, of course, going anywhere near the frontline. By late 1967, the pressure from unhappy officers had reached a level which Ojukwu could not ignore. He allowed the army to form the 'Biafran Army Service Corps' but this new organisation operated alongside the Food Directorate. For the rest of the war the two organisations would squabble over the dwindling food that was available. In an attempt to solve the food issues at a local level, some unit commanders formed any wounded soldiers who were not fit for frontline service into 'Survival Companies'. The idea was that these recovering soldiers who stayed with their units would plant crops to feed themselves and their comrades. Better organised units would also keep chickens to supply the troops with eggs as long as long as they could stop the livestock being eaten!

The Militia in 1967-1968

The initial outburst of enthusiasm for the war saw thousands of willing recruits arrive at army camps and recruiting stations and recruiting offices were totally overwhelmed by the number of volunteers coming forward. With so few weapons available to the army, most of the recruits had to be turned away and this led to frustration amongst the young men. This frustration needed to be channelled into some kind of military activity for the volunteers. As in other states at war, the obvious answer was to form a second-line territorial force or militia. The first militia force was raised in Port Harcourt and led by local businessman Joe Achuzia who was to go on

A patrol of soldiers from the elite 'S' Brigade patrol the countryside around Colonel Ojukwu's HQ as part of their role of serving as the Biafran leaders bodyguard. They have short wave radios which were in short supply in the Biafran Army throughout the war. Only a small number of Biafran soldiers would have been as well turned out as these men who all have the red lightning flash arm patch of the 'S' Brigade on their shoulders. (Author's Collection)

to serve with some distinction in the regular army. His militia quickly grew to 5,000 volunteers and before long was in competition with the other units that were soon raised. Several other cities followed the example set by Port Harcourt with the main militia forces raised in Aba, Enugu, Umhuahia and Onitsha. The other militias, apart from that from Port Harcourt, usually came under the umbrella of the 'National Militia'. The militia's expanded at a pace with both men and women being accepted into them; the volunteers were trained in the evenings and at the weekend with drill taking the form of PT and mock battles armed with wooden rifles. A lucky few had shotguns or locally made 'dane' hunting guns whilst others were issued with crudely made machetes. In scenes reminiscent of the early days of the British Home Guard in the summer of 1940, older men with real or imagined 'military' experience drilled the militiamen and taught them the rudiments of warfare.

The militia set up their own military organisation with seconded officers receiving the job of providing the volunteers with better training. University lecturers, civil servants and police officers often took on the role of trainers even though most had no military experience. Tasks given to the militia were at first strictly civil defence related, with roadblocks set up every few hundred yards in some places with the intention being to capture fifth columnists and other saboteurs. Officially, there were four main tasks given to the militia:

1. To provide reinforcements for the regular Biafran Army,
2. To perform security roles in rear areas, thus relieving regular units to stay in the frontline,
3. To garrison any recaptured 'liberated' areas of Biafra, and
4. To help to keep up public morale with parades and demonstrations as well as having a presence in general.[2]

At first, the various militia groups were independent of each other and there was little if any co-operation between them. The command system for the militia was also at first organised on a regional basis but later there were attempts to centralise it. In an effort to give the militia a distinct identity separate to the regular Biafran Army it had its own rank system introduced by its commander in 1967, General Philip Effiong, with its lowest rank being Sub-Patroller with its army equivalent 2nd Lieutenant. The rest of the ranks with their army equivalent were: Patroller – Lieutenant, Chief-Patroller – Captain, Tracker – Major and Tracker Major – Lieutenant Colonel. During the early battles of 1967 and early 1968 militia units took part in many battles and skirmishes alongside the regular army. By early 1968 most militiamen between the ages of 17 and 35 had been conscripted into the army. The militia was no longer needed and was too expensive to run so was duly disbanded shortly after the fall of Port Harcourt.

The Biafran Organisation of Freedom Fighters

As Colonel Ojukwu announced the disbandment of the Militia he also announced the formation of the 'Biafran Organisation of Freedom Fighters' (BOFF) – an armed group drafted from students and other youngsters with the aim of operating as infiltrators behind the Federal lines. Eventually, the BOFF included volunteers from the ranks of the militia that refused to join the army or to be commanded by regular officers, and former militia-officers who had had disagreements with regular military officers.

The BOFF was placed under the command of Colonel Aghanya, who was given few resources and had to raise, train and equip his units with whatever weapons were provided to his volunteers. In turn, the latter were to be chosen after a stringent screening process which would test them for intelligence and resourcefulness. Female volunteers were also welcomed and they had to undergo the same training course as their male colleagues. The volunteers first had to take part in a fitness test based on the British Outward Bound course. Although not strictly speaking a guerrilla force, the BOFF were to use guerrilla tactics: its main operational area became occupied northern Biafra, and the Mid-West region, where Federal control was often very lose.

Some of the BOFF had volunteered to work as cook-boys and servants for Federal officers, while girls were frequently taken by Nigerian units as cooks or washerwomen: both acted as spies. Of course, as the war wore on, ever more of them were uncovered and they were usually dealt with severely. Despite such dangers, there was never a shortage of volunteers for service with the BOFF, and there was no end of talent. Many of the freedom fighters were intelligent and were trained in being able to outsmart Nigerian officers and men. For example, one group of 30 BOFF volunteers operating in the Mid-West were able to convince a local Federal Army commander into handing over rifles to them. They told him that they were from a minority tribe who hated the Biafrans and wanted rifles so that they could take revenge upon them.

Although the operations launched by BOFF did add to the already well organised Biafran intelligence network, ultimately, they became too dangerous. Many BOFF volunteers were executed as

Colonel Chukwuemeka Odumegwu Ojukwu, the 34 year old leader of Biafra, inspects some his 'S' Brigade troops in the summer of 1967. He is accompanied by a drum band who are wearing the 'Fidel' style cap worn by many Biafran troops during the war. Their drums, on close inspection, are leftovers from a military band in the pre-Independence era featuring the insignia of the West African Force. Colonel Ojukwu wears dress uniform with a gold aiguillette and the white and red plume attached to the front of his peaked cap. His ADC carrying the officers dress sword appears to have removed his old Nigerian Army peaked cap badge and has not received his new Biafran cap badge. (Albert Grandolini Collection)

Soldiers guard a road as an expectant crowd wait for the arrival of their leader, Colonel Ojukwu in the early days of the civil war. They are aboard one of the Land Rovers which the Biafran Army relied on for its main transport needs. Many of these vehicles had been taken from car pools of government ministries to help out with the war effort. In most cases they arrived in the standard pre-1967 government colour scheme, yellow. After being hastily painted in a camouflage scheme they were handed over to Biafran Army units often with machineguns mounted on them. (Author's Collection)

the Nigerians became more aware and suspicious of them. Later in the war the BOFF was thus forced to switch to a 'pure' guerrilla role, and sometimes even fought alongside regular Biafran troops (see below for details).

Civil Defenders

As in other civil wars the paranoia caused by the suspected presence of Nigerian spies and saboteurs in Biafra saw the raising of a large force of Civil Defenders. These were poorly armed volunteers who spent their free time 'combing' the jungle around their villages and towns looking for 'fifth columnists'. Armed usually with machetes and other primitive weapons the Civil Defenders also set up multiple road blocks to search cars, cyclists and pedestrians for anything suspicious. No one was immune from the searches by the Civil Defenders, including Biafran government officials and army officers. Many hundreds, if not thousands, of 'innocent' civilians were beaten up and some were killed by the volunteers who found the slightest thing suspicious. By July 1967 the total number of Civil Defenders reached 50,000 with only a handful having firearms of any kind. Even though the roadblocks they set up around a town or village were sometimes within sight of each other, it did no good to protest that you had been searched a few minutes beforehand. Roadblocks were usually organised in a chicane system which made it difficult for vehicles to manoeuvre around. The Civil Defenders tended to guard a particular roadblock and became quite territorial. Few real saboteurs were found but many innocent people, especially amongst the minorities of Biafra, suffered because of them.

Biafran paranoia included the fear of non-existent Nigerian paratroopers and the Civil Defenders were given the job of watching the skies for them. Open areas of land were often staked with sharpened sticks and gory leaflets showing Nigerian paratroopers impaled on them were distributed. Any surviving paratroopers were, according to the Ministry of Information leaflet, to be killed with bows and arrows, clubs, or knives, and women encouraged to take the fore. The fact that Nigeria had no paratroopers does not seem to have figured in the thinking of the Biafran propaganda. As the war dragged on most able bodied male Civil Defenders were conscripted into the Biafran Army. It was then left to the older volunteers and women to continue combing and other operations until the end of the war. As the war dragged on many Civil Defenders had enough to worry about other than searching for non-existent fifth columnists. In many villages and towns they did continue to set aside one day a week for 'combing' the area for saboteurs until the end of the war.

Chapter 2
Biafran Army at War

When the war began, the recruiting centres in Biafra were inundated with enthusiastic volunteers clamouring to fight the 'Vandals'.[1] Many volunteers camped outside recruitment centres in order to be first in the queue to join up. Some were motivated by wanting revenge for the treatment meted out to their relatives in northern Nigeria in 1966. Many were excited by the idea of going to war much as the volunteers in the First World War had been in August 1914. They also had a collective overconfidence that in their eyes meant that they would soon defeat the Nigerians. The first disappointment for these volunteers was that there were simply not enough weapons to go around and thousands were sent home. Most joined the ranks of the militia or the Civil Defenders and waited for more rifles to arrive from abroad as they had been promised by Ojukwu. In the early months of 1968 there were still plenty of volunteers and at some recruitment centres they whittled them down. If 200 volunteers came forward they were sent on a 2-mile run with the first 20 across the line being recruited. As the war dragged on the defeats of mid-1968 meant that the initial enthusiasm for the war began to wane. The reality of the war and its dangers began to dawn on all but the most patriotic recruits. Reports from relatives who were fighting began to get back to their villages and casualties were beginning to fill local hospitals. The lack of weaponry, uniforms and equipment gave volunteers little confidence in what awaited them at the front. One source of experienced recruits for the Biafrans were the Second World War veterans who had fought in Burma in 1944 – 45. A large number of these veterans were recruited into the Nigerian Army but there were far fewer veterans available to join the Biafran Army. Although a useful addition to the ranks, the fact that the veterans were allowed to join the army at their previous rank caused issues. As with the Nigerian veterans, the Biafran veterans were frustrated by the lack of organisation in the army. Assimilating them into a largely amateur fighting force was always going to cause problems and the arrogance of some veterans didn't help matters.

Basic Training

Once they had signed up for the army the average Biafran recruit received only the most basic of training. This usually involved a period of three to four weeks marching up and down the parade ground singing patriotic songs and carrying wooden rifles. During the war, however, the amount of training that recruits were given dropped to as low as 4 days, though most received at least 14 days, but this included several days of the wasteful square bashing. With so few weapons available at the frontline the recruits had to train with carved wooden rifles or sticks. They were lucky if they even got sight of a real rifle and those weapons that were at the training camps were kept safely in the instructors' hands. Before he reached the frontline, the recruit would certainly not get to fire a rifle and not surprisingly target practice was unheard of. Square bashing was conducted by officers whose orders were shouted in accents often straight out of Sandhurst. To the average young Biafran recruit coming from a rural village these educated officers must have seemed totally alien to them. Their enthusiasm to learn how to fight the hated 'vandals' however meant that they were keen to receive any kind of military training and performed their parade ground 'left about turns' and 'right about turns' with gusto. Mock battle training did take place, again with wooden rifles but this often had little relevance to the situation facing the recruits when they reached the front. The journalist Michael Leapman wrote a report in July 1969 describing the experience of new recruits at the front: 'Here the boys with fake wooden rifles, move deftly through the undergrowth, always ending by annihilating the enemy absolutely.' In describing their anti-tank training, he said: 'They learn how to line up one of Nigeria's British built armoured cars in the sights of

This iconic photograph by Italian journalist Romano Cagnoni shows newly arrived recruits at the Okigwi Training Camp. As his original caption says they would receive scant training and be issued with whatever rifles or other weapons were available. After their two weeks of obstacle courses and marching on the parade ground they would be sent to the front. Most would have only been able to watch their instructor handle a real gun and the chances are it would be a different type then they were issued with later. (Romano Cagnoni)

At a training camp these determined looking recruits have nothing but roughly carved wooden rifles to practice their military skills with. They were given plenty of advice of how to act when they reached the frontline but very little practical training. These young men have not been issued with any uniform at this stage and they would be lucky to get a shirt, trousers and boots. Some would be issued with the rising sun shoulder patch which they would then have to attach to their own shirts. (Author's Collection)

Young Biafran recruits march around the parade ground in the summer of 1968 carrying their sticks in lieu of the rifles they might one day receive. The looks on the young men's faces show their varying attitudes to what was by then often being press ganged into the army. Most show determination to fight for their beleaguered country while others look as if they wish they were somewhere else. (Author's Collection)

their French made bazookas. Then after just three weeks they head for the front line, where things are not all the same.' In the same article Leapman added:

> In military terms it is a poor joke of a war......Sandhurst training is fine for officers who can count on a fair level of competence among their men, or alternatively who do not have any wars to fight. It gives few clues to the handling of illiterate, inexperienced boys, fresh from the villages, understandably terrified at the sound of gunfire.[2]

As the war situation grew graver in 1968 many troops were sent to the front with little or no training and no rifles. Essentially, they were dumped on frontline units. The idea was that if they spent some time at the front, then when rifles did become available, they would already be used to daily shelling and other dangers. Some may have drifted away and would have been allowed to leave by the veterans as they were simply in the way. Desertion was, as in any army, a serious offence but officers often turned a blind eye to it when they could not give the new recruits a rifle to fire. After the disastrous campaigns of the summer of 1968 the high casualty rate meant that a large number of replacements were needed. In order to keep the flow of recruits constant it was decided to introduce conscription from August 1968 by issuing quotas to village headmen to fill. When this system did not provide enough recruits units sent out press gangs to take suitable men off the streets. These recruitment units targeted dance halls and cinemas and took young men away to the training camps. Officers in civilian clothing were not spared and had to convince the recruiting sergeants that they were already serving. These pressed recruits were always going to make worse soldiers than their volunteer comrades. Their presence at the front affected the morale of the other soldiers who, being bored and hungry, were more likely to listen to their grumbling.

It soon became obvious to visiting journalists that the 17 to 35 age limits for recruits were no longer being adhered to. Teenagers of 13 to 15 years old began to appear in the frontline: many were simply homeless and attached themselves to units so that they could get food and shelter. Some of the older teenagers had been turned away from the recruiting centres in 1967 and early 1968 for being underage: they had returned to the same bases several times while others had travelled many miles to try their luck at more distanced centres. Some recruiting officers were prepared to take in the more capable under-age volunteers who often were made to prove their worth. This even involved physical tests with one recruit being admitted to the army after beating adults in a 100 metres race! Once the boys were at the front they were sometimes seen as a liability by their adult comrades. Despite the enthusiasm shown by youngsters they rarely had the maturity they needed when the fighting began. Unit commanders had to make do with the inexperienced young recruits and try to mould them into good soldiers. Colonel Achuzia told a visiting Canadian reporter to the Owerri front, Peter Worthington (a veteran of the Korean War): 'You'll not find this like Korea, these soldiers are no good. Children, remnants, they're all we can get. You can't call them soldiers at all. Well we do what we can….' After Worthington had defended the young soldiers, mostly teenagers, who made up the unit Achuzia went on, 'They are children. With real soldiers I'd be past Owerri by now and heading for Port Harcourt. These people I have to bully, to chase, to frighten into battle. I have to make them more frightened of me than they are of the enemy'.[3]

Route marches were usually part of the training and these men have been given a mixture of Lee Enfield and Mauser rifles to carry. Rifles issued to recruits during training were often damaged beyond repair or were models that had run out of ammunition. Because the Biafran Army had so many types of rifle in service it was an impossible task to replace some ammunition once the initial supply that arrived with the guns had run out. (Author's Collection)

Once at the front, the young and often unarmed recruits were expected to hang around with the older soldiers waiting for a rifle to become available. The naturally adventurous youths were likely to get themselves killed before they had a chance to fight by exposing themselves to enemy fire. Others ignored advice from older, experienced soldiers – usually with fatal consequences. One official communiqué put some of this advice into typical official jargon regarding withdrawing under fire: 'Be very tactically aware and know when to withdraw…the fool dies, the tactically aware survive.'

A group of bare-chested Biafran recruits get 'aiming' lessons with the similarly dressed instructor in the city of Umuahia. He is armed with a Czech vz. 58 assault rifle while his pupils are 'armed' with crudely carved sticks. Few Biafran volunteers ever got to handle or even touch a real rifle before going off to the frontline. Hopefully when they eventually got their hands on a rifle or other firearm they would be given at least a brief introduction to the weapon. (Author's Collection)

With the war situation worsening the age of youngsters got lower with even 10-year-olds being issued with the rifles. Boys as young as seven were at the frontline and carried ammunition and acted as assistants to their more mature comrades. Boys of 10 to 14 years were often recruited into 'reconnaissance battalions' which were really units of child spies. After a short training course they were sent into Federal camps to hang around and make friends with the Nigerian soldiers. If they managed to ingratiate themselves with the enemy troops by doing chores and fetching and carrying they could gather intelligence. When they had got enough information they would run away from the camp and try and make their way back to 'friendly' lines to report on unit strengths or similar matters. This was obviously dangerous work and the Federal troops often became aware of the boys' intentions. There were reports of the Nigerian soldiers meting out justice to these 'traitors' and the practice became unpopular with all but the most ruthless Biafran commanders. Officially, adult soldiers were aged between 17 or 18 and 35, while between the ages of 12 and 17 they were classed as 'big boys'. Any younger soldiers were simply defined as being 'boys' with most between 9 and 11.

Young recruits watch one of their comrades examine a Czech vz. 52 semi-automatic rifle during their basic training. This rudimentary familiarising of troops with rifles was useful to a point for soldiers who had often never seen a gun. The fact was that when they got to the front they would be issued with a different type of rifle when one eventually became available. (Albert Grandolini Collection)

Five Biafran soldiers sit outside their bunker reinforced with tree trunks which they have built in the rain forest. Defensive positions like this were constructed as part of the defence lines on the approaches to Biafran held towns and villages. With little heavy weaponry available trench systems like this often had to be defended by a handful of troops. In many cases there were no machineguns or other heavier weaponry available and their Mauser rifles had to suffice. At times the Biafran troops were down to 1 or 2 bullets per man and 3 was the standard ration when on the defensive like these men. (Private Collection)

Colonel Joe 'Hannibal' Achuzia, the enigmatic and controversial Biafran commander, is pictured wearing a standard army peaked cap with a duck hunter camouflage jacket. Achuzia was an ex-Engineer and former Militia officer who transferred to the regular army after the first few months of the war. He had some success with his 'gung ho' but costly tactics which meant that he sometimes had to enforce discipline with his revolver. Achuzia freely admitted to shooting deserters or 'cowards' who refused to go into action and said that these measures were necessary in times of war. Some said that it was the fact that his men were more frightened of him than they were of the enemy! (Private Collection)

Biafran Army Officers

The officers who had to command the Biafran army during the civil war were the usual mix of good, bad and indifferent. What made the job of the Biafran army officer more stressful was that they were commanding men who were largely untrained, poorly armed, badly dressed and hungry. The Biafran army had a small hard-core of officers when it was formed with a total of 5 lieutenant-colonels, 16 majors, 15 captains, 17 lieutenants and 40 second lieutenants. Their total increased to 330 in January 1967, of which 93 had survived the July coup.

Biafran officers came from two main sources. Most used to serve with the Nigerian army. Out of these, only 8 had staff training (such as received at Camberley), and had been taught the skills necessary to administer an armed force, and an idea of strategy. This in turn meant that lots of lower-ranking officers and NCOs had to be promoted, and although they proved able to perform in the field, they usually lacked the important backroom skills. The situation worsened by late 1967, by when the number of well-trained officers had been reduced to three, after Major Nzeogwu was killed in action and two others – Lieutenant-Colonel Banjo and Major Ifeaiuna – were executed on orders from Ojukwu; lieutenant-colonels Imo, Ogunewe and Njoku lost their posts in literal witch-hunts by the politicians and the public in the aftermath of military defeats (some where even attacked by angry mobs and had to flee for their lives, taking shelter with fellow officers until things calmed down). The reason for a such situation was quite obvious: from Ojukwu's standpoint, it was important to explain these early setbacks as 'unexpected' failures and find and punish the scapegoats as he could not admit his own failures – especially not after all of his pre-war boasting about the prowess of the Biafran armed forces. However, Ojukwu's paranoia and mistrust persisted, fuelling this fire and the practice of accusing officers of being saboteurs and at later times as traitors.

Unsurprisingly, replacing experienced officers with those untainted by the military intrigue of 1966 took time. The first step was to set up a Training Depot in the old Enugu Jail buildings and the Hilltop Officers Cadet School on the outskirts of the capital. It is doubtful if many trainees completed the full course as the need for them was rapidly growing. When the war began there were just about enough officers to go around – at a time when the entire armed forces counted a mere few thousand. As the army was expanded to about 40,000 men, most officer-training courses had to be cut short and cadets forced to complete their training in the field. Luckily for the Biafrans, the average young easterner had a higher level of education than those from the rest of Nigeria. This meant that more of them were capable of absorbing their training if they were allowed to complete it before being sent to their units. Officers should have been given 4 to 6 weeks of training, depending on the war situation, though many went to the front with only a few weeks training. The officers who were posted to the front without proper training had to 'learn on the job' and therefore suffered a high proportion of casualties. Barely trained junior officers arrived at the front full of bravado and often tried to prove themselves, with fatal results. Many were killed within a few days of getting to the front and quite often within a few hours of taking up their command. In an effort to prove themselves to veteran soldiers and NCOs they didn't take the time to acclimatise themselves to frontline conditions and dangers and were too proud to listen to advice. This high attrition rate explains why a staggering 10,000 new officers were trained during the war. Out of this total almost one in three, or 3,000, died and by the end of the war the Biafrans were running out of suitable candidates. General Effiong summed up the officer shortages by saying, 'Unlike the Nigerian officers my officers led every attack. They go in first like Israelis, it's the only way we know, even though we have lost some of our best men in this way.'[4]

When the militia and its officers were absorbed into the regular Biafran Army in early 1968 the dynamics of the officer corps changed. The incoming ex-militia officers were supposed to get a crash course in their new role as regular officers, but many did not. Many of these 'amateur' officers had learnt their trade at the front commanding militia units with few if any weapons. Their 'gung-ho' attitude came from the fact that they had learned to fight using their own initiative. Now under the more stringent control of the regular army many were often frustrated by the orders of their regular army colleagues. The militia officers regarded the more experienced officers as 'stuffy' and as taking too much notice of military protocol. They also accused many regular officers of boasting continuously about their service with the United Nations in the Congo between 1960 and 1963. According to the new officers their war service had involved some low-level skirmishing against poorly armed Congolese irregulars! The regular army officers were of course heavily influenced by their training at staff colleges. This training emphasised the carrying out of orders to the letter and initiative was not regarded as a virtue. To the former militia officers having to work within the constraints of the regular army just stifled initiative and frustrated their natural way of fighting. In their turn the regular army officers regarded the new arrivals as 'schoolboy upstarts'. They did grudgingly acknowledge their bravery in some of the early battles of the war but bemoaned their lack of training. Some officers complained that the lack of formal training left them unprepared for large unit operations and it was said that they had little or no concept of what preparations were necessary before going into action. Maps were rarely consulted and little or no reconnaissance of enemy positions was undertaken by many officers. Some ex-militia officers like Colonel Achuzia preferred to do their own reconnaissance, even if it involved moving in disguise through enemy positions and observing their strengths. Achuzia performed his own reconnaissance on several occasions by wandering through them in tattered civilian clothing and a stick. He chatted to the Nigerian soldiers who saw him as a harmless and quite amusing old man just passing through their camp. Achuzia's dangerous work was helped by the fact that he did indeed look just like the wizened old man he was playing.

Whether the officer was a time served regular or a new militia officer they were still influenced by the 'spit and polish' of their senior officers. Colonel Ojukwu himself was a graduate of Eaton Hall Officer Cadet School and was loathe to adapt his tactics to the situation his army was facing. However, his strategy of fighting the Nigerian Army with conventional tactics put the Biafrans at a disadvantage: outgunned and outnumbered the Biafran army could not hope to sustain conventional warfare against the Federal army for long. Ojukwu was in a way a prisoner of his Sandhurst-style military education and shared this attitude with many of his similarly trained officers. As one scathing correspondent said 'If he had read Mao rather than General Sir Douglas Haig, he might have won.'

A Biafran soldier helps his 'shell shocked' comrade to the rear where he may have time to recover before being sent back into action. Just like the soldiers on the Western Front in the First World War the Biafrans had to endure long bombardments from the Federal artillery. In Biafra the mental breakdown caused by sustained periods under shell fire was called appropriately 'Artillery Sickness'. (Romano Cagnoni)

General Effiong, the Biafran Army Chief of Staff followed similar ideas to his leader. He was described as looking like a 'British Staff General' with '...a polished Sam Browne belt, a sword for ceremonial occasions and a chauffeur-driven car with a general's flag.' Effiong's officers were similarly described as having: 'moustaches, swagger sticks, batmen and officer's messes.'[5]

Some journalists found the attitude of the 'spit and polish' Biafran officers either tragic or amusing. The latter was little surprising: these immaculately turned out officers with swagger sticks regularly commanded units consisting of boys with no shoes, holes in the seats of their trousers, and a tree branch in lieu of a rifle.

Frontline and Staff Officers

One thing that field officers, no matter what their background, could agree on was their total lack of respect for the staff officers

A comrade or friend of a wounded soldier carries him back to an aid station on his back along a village path. Without a proper medical service in the Biafran Army it was fate whether a wounded man survived or not. The Biafran soldiers earned a reputation for being stoical when injured but the reality for most injured troops was grim. In one news reel from a wounded man being carried to the rear repeats the same phrase, "I will not die of a Vandal (Nigerian) bullet!" (Author's Collection)

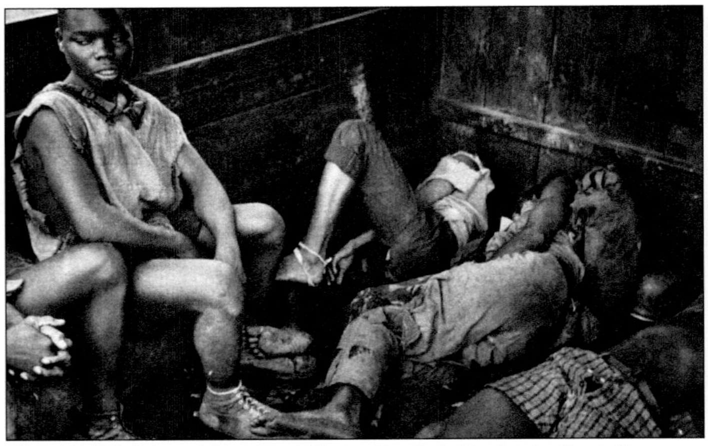

Wounded Biafran soldiers sit and lay patiently in the back of a civilian lorry waiting to be taken to the hospital. To save precious fuel the driver will have been instructed not to take them for treatment until the truck is full. In the heat of the Nigerian jungle infections could soon get into open wounds and the delay in getting them to the hospital could be a death sentence (Romano Cagnoni)

at headquarters. Army command posts became notorious as places for battle-shy officers to hide with their retinue of bodyguards, orderlies, provosts and runners. These posts were often far from the front and were carefully camouflaged against air raids amongst trees and undergrowth. From these remote posts the officers issued contradictory and often confusing orders to frontline commanders. Field officers complained that orders issued from the staff officers' 'hideaways' were usually out of date by the time they reached their positions. Staff officers were loath to visit the front because they knew that to do so would risk being kept there to replace dead or wounded officers. With little or no concept of what was going on in the one-sided war against the Nigerians they kept sending poorly armed units into suicidal assaults. Certainly enough, there is resentment – even hostility – between frontline- and staff-officers in every army, especially one at war. However, because of the dire situation in Biafra this common resentment reached new levels, and this was unsurprising because the frontline-officers were suffering alongside their men, from hunger, cold and discomfort.

Frontline officers also usually shared the same risks as their soldiers – including their high casualty rate – while those serving in the rear command posts were living a relatively easy life. Indeed, many spent their evenings and weekends partying with their girlfriends or prostitutes in the comfort of their barracks.

As the high casualty rate amongst the frontline officers grew it became harder for staff officers to stay away from the front. Unsurprisingly, staff officers used every trick they could to remain at their rear positions and continue performing their 'vital work'. Despite appeals from Ojukwu and his 'fighting' commanders for these officers to get involved they did all they could to avoid this.

Another complaint from the field officers was the lack of promotion being gained by the junior officers. Promotions of officers in the field – and they included many former students and ex-militia officers – occurred very slowly. For example, despite the high casualty rate amongst junior officers, the highest rank attained by an ex-student officer in the field was that of a major. Many complained that all the available promotions were being given to the "layabouts" and other hangers-on at rear command posts.

Another worrying trend during the war was the way in which charlatans could gain officer ranks they were not qualified for. Applicants were supposed to have a high school level of education but a number of unqualified men played the system: some were criminals who were used to conning people and bluffed their way into training colleges. In the chaos of the war, they found it relatively easy to flout the rules. No doubt, many of these were so-called 'hot heads': people willing to risk their lives (and those of their troops) to gain a position they could never reach in civilian life. Once they were in command some used their new status to abuse their men and to steal supplies from them. In the 'survival of the fittest' atmosphere which pervaded Biafra during the war it was easy to take advantage of the situation – and most of the officers did: corruption in general and the black market in particular were rife during the civil war, giving these bogus officers plenty of opportunities to take advantage.

Biafran officers of course were the typical mixture of good and bad seen in most armies in the 20th century. The shortages that soldiers endured on the frontline, of food and comforts, often caused breakdowns in the relationship between those in command and their troops. Ordinary soldiers in the trenches were well aware of the difference in lifestyle between their officers and themselves. Some officers managed to get regular supplies of cigarettes and alcohol as well as the women to keep them entertained, but many were rarely seen anywhere near the frontlines.

Certainly enough, the primary reason why most officers would not share such luxuries with their men was that there was not enough to go around. On average, troops were happy to share one cigarette and a glass of locally-made gin between 5-6 of them; a mere 90 uniforms were usually issued to a brigade – at least 30 of which were handed out to the staff officers and other hangers-on; while officers wore full uniforms, most of the troops wore rags. With the relatives of some commanders being employed as ADCs and in other staff roles, the fact that they got full uniforms while their men froze at night in their trenches caused great resentment.

As in any war the best and worst was brought out by the civil war, with both sides having plenty of heroes and plenty of villains. On the Biafran side however, the fact that officers were under constant pressure from July 1967 until January 1970 made the job harder. To keep fighting for 30 months while commanding boys with few rifles and often no bullets, their continued resistance was quite astounding.

Religious Influence

At the start of the war the largely Christian population of Biafra was pious, 'god fearing' and attended church every Sunday. When the army went to war it was not surprising that they were joined by scores of clergymen who acted as chaplains and because they frequently joined troops in the trenches, there were a number of fatalities amongst these Biafran clergymen.

In the desperate situation of the last year of the war many Biafran soldiers came under the influence of local juju men, soothsayers and spiritualists. The most prominent of these religious leaders was 'Doctor Wise' whose influence even affected the military decisions made by officers under his spell. His power over the traditionally superstitious soldiers and their officers was frequently compared to that of Rasputin upon the family of the last Russian Czar, and it often undermined the chain-of-command.

Soldiers bought charms from the juju men which were supposed to make them immune to bullets. Of course, the real value of the charms would soon be seen, but troops were desperate for anything that might help them and clutched at straws. Officers were not immune to the promises of the spiritualists either and even recruited them onto their staffs officially as chaplains. They were given a salary and accommodation and had the ears of the officers making important strategic decisions. It was reported that the 12th Division in particular was adversely affected by the activities of the spiritualists. The effect on the division's morale was largely blamed for its collapse in December 1969 and January 1970. Although spiritualism was not confined to the Biafran army the majority of Nigerian soldiers were either Muslim or Animists and were not under the same amount of religious influence as the Biafrans were. As the expected victors of the fighting they did not need the 'crutch' of religion to cling to as the Biafran soldiers did.

Life at the Front

Away from the main battles and offensives of the civil war there were long periods of little or no military activity in some sectors. As in any conflict there were quiet periods and quiet sectors where the life at the front was tedious and when there was no fighting a sort of routine soon developed. Even when the war situation was quiet the Nigerian artillery opened the day with a morning bombardment. At a particular time in the morning the Federal artillery would fire off a few rounds in the general direction of Biafran trenches. This 'good morning' barrage as it was called was reported to be used as an alarm clock by the Biafrans and usually did little harm to the defenders. Biafrans became used to being under bombardment and became hardened to the inconvenience of spending hours in their bunkers. As the war wore on, some Biafran soldiers became accustomed to coming under heavy fire. As one journalist said, the troops who would at one time have 'cut and run' now 'hunkered down' in their bunkers and held on as long as possible. One small unit he visited had suffered 600 rounds of 81mm mortar fire in a single morning and had held on to their positions. Other soldiers were, however, badly affected by shell shock which was widely known in Biafra as 'artillery sickness'. Their comrades who had to deal with soldiers with this trauma called the mentally damaged troops 'artillery boys'. In the Biafran army the level of shell shock was probably high because for many soldiers their first contact with modern technology was the first time they were shelled. Some had not even been able to hear the sound of a rifle being fired during training, so the terror of coming under shell fire was multiplied. Fake shell shock also became an issue with groups of youths who had deserted their units roaming around the bush. They would travel from food station to food station showing the classic symptoms of 'artillery sickness.' It soon became known that these charlatans were faking it and they were given short shrift. The stress of living for long periods in trenches a few hundred yards from the enemy was bound to affect soldiers. Often the Biafran and Nigerian lines were a matter of yards apart with one journalist remembering being only 30 yards from Federal trenches. He was supposed to be reassured when a Biafran lieutenant told him: 'The closer you are, the safer you are, don't be afraid.' As the lieutenant explained 'when you are so close to the enemy their shots go over your head, usually.'[6]

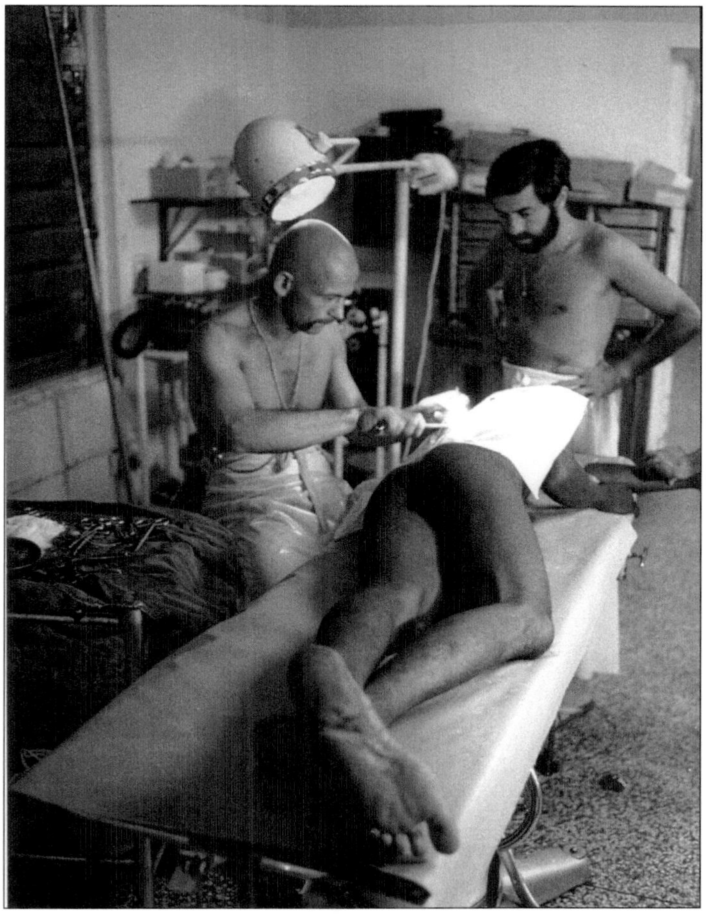

International volunteer doctors work on a wounded Biafran soldier at one of the main hospitals. The plight of the Biafrans attracted support from a large number of international medical and other charities. Although volunteer doctors did great work many soldiers did not reach the main hospitals in time for help. (Author's Collection)

One obsession for the Biafran soldier was avoiding being wounded as even a slight wound could mean death. Although

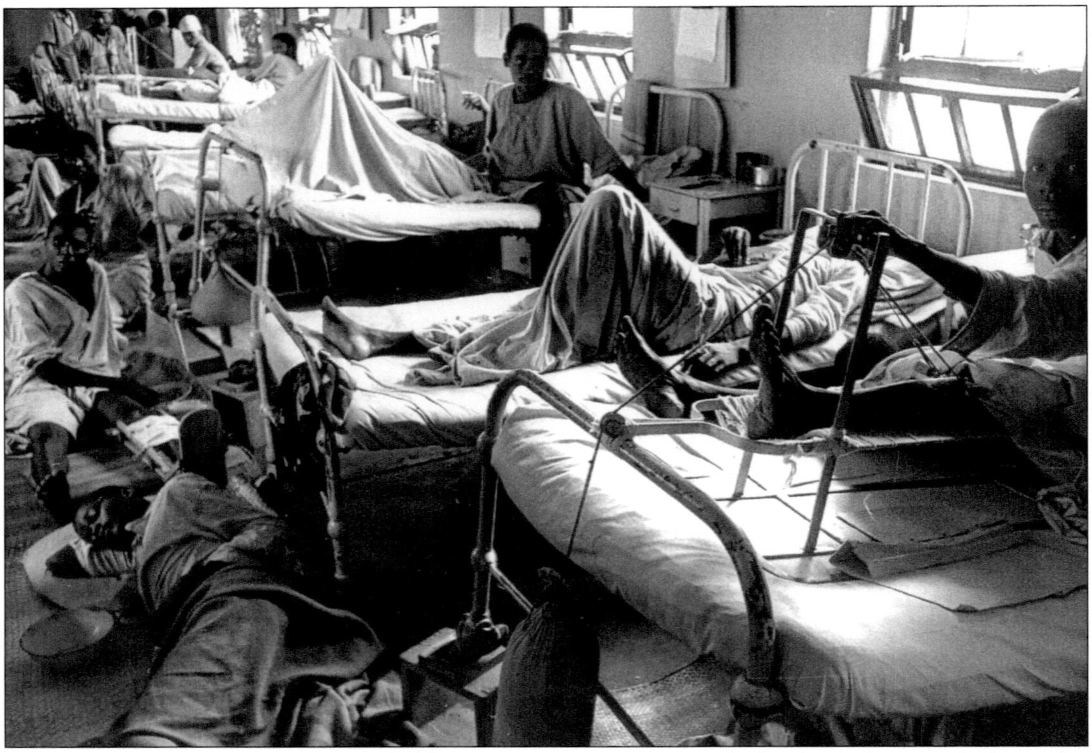

Biafran wounded lie in a recovery ward with the lucky ones getting a bed while their less lucky comrades lay on the floor. All of these men are the fortunate ones who have managed to get back from the front for treatment. Some of the medicine the soldiers received was very good but there were never enough beds available in military or civilian hospitals for the wounded. (Author's Collection)

Wounded soldiers rest under the veranda of the Queen Elizabeth Hospital in Umhuahia in March 1968. All military and civilian hospitals were overcrowded and these men have at least been given beds for their recuperation. These men may have been lucky to survive a delay of 36 to 48 hours from being wounded to getting medical attention. A soldier's survival often depended on the type of injury he received and the availability of scarce transport. (Author's Collection)

medical facilities at Biafra's main hospitals were comparatively good, a soldier's first problem was to reach them without dying. Biafran soldiers who were lightly wounded were often expected to make their own way back to the rear areas. If they were lucky a few of their comrades would carry them on stretchers to the rear or on their heads like porters. It could often be a 30-mile journey back to the nearest hospital and in many cases complications like gangrene or blood poisoning had already affected the casualties before they got there. Biafran doctors became adept at dealing with infected wounds caused by delays in getting the wounded examined. In most cases they had no choice but to amputate an arm or leg to save the soldiers' lives. Stomach wounds or injuries to the internal organs usually meant a death sentence for the soldier. Even when there were motor vehicles available to take them to the military hospital they would have to wait until nightfall due to the Nigerian air attacks on any trucks in daytime. Getting soldiers who had been wounded in the stomach, or other internal organs, to the hospital was particularly important. In the tropical heat a stomach wound could turn gangrenous within in a few hours and the wounded man was certain to die.

The Biafrans suffered a high proportion of head wounds due to their soldiers' habit of crawling towards Nigerian positions without helmets. Nigerian defenders would simply spray the undergrowth with copious amounts of ammunition. This meant that the two sides often never came close to each other as the thick jungle obscured their view and would depend on the cries of the wounded or the shouts of officers calling for a withdrawal to know if they had been successful in repelling an attack.

The Problem of Fraternisation

At the start of the war, and in the wake of the anti-Ibo massacres in northern Nigeria, the Biafran soldiers thirsted for revenge against the 'vandals.' As was often the case this hatred gradually abated amongst some soldiers and a mutual respect developed on both sides. When soldiers were facing each other in trenches only a few hundred yards apart a degree of fraternisation developed. Local truces were arranged and the Nigerians would send goodwill gestures of food and others supplies to the Biafrans. In exchange they would be asked for items such as the Cuban-style field cap with rising sun badge which were highly prized souvenirs for the Nigerians. At the Onitsha front, where some of the fiercest fighting of the war went on, a local agreement was arranged. This truce allowed the opposing units to bathe and sunbathe on opposite banks of the river. At other times games of football were even arranged between the units with the agreement of their officers. As with fraternisation throughout military history, when they found out about it some officers stopped it. Other more relaxed officers turned a blind eye or even helped organise the exchange of goods between the units. On at least one occasion fraternisation led to the coming over to the Biafran side of Federal troops. In August 1968, a Nigerian unit of 3 officers and

98 other ranks deserted their positions and joined the Biafran unit facing them. Their commander said he and his men had spent time talking to the Biafrans and got on well with them and so they all decided to go over to them.

Army Discipline

Discipline at the front was often harshly enforced with draconian punishments, such as floggings, for refusing to obey orders. Soldiers were often beaten with long canes in a punishment that was as humiliating to the victim as well as painful. Punishment was always administered in front of their comrades to add to the humiliation and their cries of pain were often greeted with derision by the other men. Achuzia ordered soldiers who he had left their units without permission to 25 lashes of the cane on several occasions. He also pistol-whipped men on the battlefield for a number of 'minor' indiscretions in an attempt to spread fear to the other troops. Desertion or cowardice under fire officially carried the death penalty but it was at the discretion of the officer with some taking the soldiers' age or experience into account. It was often left up to the commander to administer the punishment in person and the mercenary Taffy Williams was reported to have personally shot six deserters with his revolver. Colonel Achuzia also admitted to the press that he shot deserters in May 1968 as the only means to keep the troops at the front. Rapists were often punished by death, especially as their victims were usually Ibo women or were from one of the minority tribes. Officers like Achuzia were strict to say the least but they gained the respect of their men by their actions at the front. Achuzia was admired even by the soldiers who feared him and had a reputation for being incorruptible. Such officers were hard on their own men but were even more draconian with any prisoners who were taken. Achuzia ordered that no Nigerian prisoners were to be taken and made sure that this rule was obeyed at all times. Although most of his troops feared him, he still had to deal with insubordination from his men. He received reports that a company of troops in a quiet sector at Aboh-Kwale Axis had mutinied; they had refused to obey their captain and were now being led by their sergeant-major who allowed them to loot, kidnap and rape the population. The Colonel got in his Land Rover with a small escort and drove to the bush HQ of the company. His convoy was ambushed and during the ensuing shootout with the mutineers he shot the RSM and then rounded up six other ringleaders. He gathered the locals who had suffered at their hands and had all the guilty soldiers shot by firing squad as an example.[7]

Biafran Tactics

The tactics of the Biafran army during the civil war were constantly governed by their inferiority in weaponry. Even when more small arms arrived in 1968, the lack of heavy weaponry – especially heavy artillery – constantly hampered them. Their inferiority in firepower, compared to the Nigerian Federal Army, meant they had to use any available means of concealment and make use of cover; moreover, it resulted in a situation where for most of the war the Biafrans were on the defensive waiting for the Nigerians to launch one of their offensives.

One advantage that the Biafrans did have was their engineers' skill in preparing defensive positions. Because any Nigerian attack was always proceeded by heavy bombardment from 105mm field guns, they frequently had to endure heavy shelling: unsurprisingly, good field fortifications – and bunkers in particular – proved essential. Of course, as with everything else, the Biafrans were short on the necessary equipment and materials: but when materials

Dick Tiger, the World Light Heavyweight boxing champion, was an ardent supporter of the Biafran cause and joined the Army in 1968 as a Lieutenant . He spent most of the war training recruits in PT and acting as a propaganda vehicle for the Biafrans. Tiger was allowed to take a break from military service to take part in the defence of his title in 1969. When the fighting started the vast majority of eminent easterners supported the Biafran cause and helped in any way they could. (Author's Collection)

were available their engineers could construct very good trench systems with bomb-proof concrete bunkers and pill-boxes. When there was less material they had to make do with a bunker dug out of the ground with tree trunks on top. With little or no barbed wire available, the only means of protecting the approaches to the trenches were sharpened wooden stakes. These 'punji sticks' were placed in large numbers in front of their trenches to slow down the attacking Nigerians.

On a few occasions the Biafrans also dug trenches in front of their defensive positions and filled them with crude oil: as a last resort these would be set on fire when the Nigerians attacked. Of course, once the oil burned out, such obstacles became useless. When the Biafrans had time to construct their defences properly they were well built as was the case with the defences around Port Harcourt. An eyewitness said that these included concrete pillboxes and well-camouflaged bunkers. The Biafrans also constructed 'jungle bunkers' on the approaches to a town or village and these would be defended by a handful of soldiers. In many sectors a sort of jungle Western Front developed with opposition trenches and bunkers a few hundred yards apart. The Nigerians always knew that their Biafran neighbours only had a few rounds to spare and tried to goad them into wasting these. To counter such tactics, the Biafrans would bang pots and pans and shout to create the illusion of well manned defences. They also built rattles like those used by football fans on the terraces in the 1950s and 1960s which – when whirled around – sounded like machinegun fire. Other similar devices were made from corrugated iron which had a stick run up and down it to produce the same effect. Drummers were also able to produce a similar sound but to what extent this fooled the Federal troops in not known. Finally, the Biafrans tried to fool the Nigerians as to the number of casualties they had suffered. It was common practice to move all their dead from the battlefield after an engagement, as did the Nigerians. In September 1969, Nigerian Major Isemede said that his troops had found 'many bloody spots but no Biafran bodies' adding with a shrug; 'we drag our casualties away and they do the same.'[8]

Whenever the Biafrans managed to stop the Nigerian advance before this got to within range of their defences, they were at advantage. The Federal army usually approached a town or village defended by the Biafrans along main roads, or smaller jungle roads, with armoured cars and armoured personnel carriers in front acting as their 'teeth arm'. Because most of the latter were wheeled, they possessed only limited cross-country capability (truth to be said, the terrain was often problematic enough that even tracked vehicles cold not pass).[9]

To stop such armoured vehicles as Saladin and Ferret armoured cars, the Biafrans often dug so-called 'elephant traps' at the side of a road. These were expertly camouflaged, often by placing abandoned cars on top of them, and although the Nigerians became wary of these tactics, they continued losing vehicles to such traps until the end of the war.

In other cases, the Biafrans would just chop down a tree and lay it across the road: this was usually enough to stop any advance as the Nigerians did not like advancing without support of their armoured cars. At other times the RAP produced a large number of homemade mines and Molotov Cocktails to throw at Federal vehicles from the bush. The famous Obunigwe (see Chapter 4) was very effective when positioned to fire down the road onto advancing columns.

Despite all such measures, sometimes there was no other way to stop an advancing Nigerian column other than to ambush its armoured cars from the surrounding jungle. Typical Biafran tactics were to let the forward escort vehicles pass before attacking soft-skin trucks and Land Rovers coming up behind. If timed well, the ambush could leave the main column isolated by blocking the road behind the armoured vehicles, even more so if – as happened often enough – the armour-crews continued to their destination while leaving their comrades behind.

The danger for the Biafrans was that the Nigerian soldiers usually had more than enough ammunition to defoliate the surrounding jungle. When ambushes became more common the trigger-happy Federal troops would simply fire off thousands of rounds into suspected sites for potential Biafran attacks.

The longer the war went on, the less afraid the Biafrans became of the Ferrets, Saladins and AMLs. On the contrary, they began actively stalking smaller patrols of these: they would search for ways to stop the vehicles, then assault them and clamber aboard them from all sides.[10] If possible, the Biafrans sought to capture the armoured vehicles intact; alternatively, they would pour fuel onto the vehicle and set them on fire, then wait for the crew to abandon them.

The Biafran engineers became experts in demolition: they not only blew up a large number of bridges during Nigerian advances, but sometimes mined them. Many rivers and creeks, especially in the southern part of Biafra were thus converted into major obstacles for the Nigerians. A Biafran engineer busy fastening dynamite while interviewed, explained: 'If the North invades they are going to have to swim every river in the region.'[11]

Much of the dynamite used by the Biafran engineers was confiscated from industrial suppliers in the south of Biafra. They also learned to use the weather to their advantage: the best examples for this are known from the rain season of 1969, when the majority of tracks and roads became quagmires. The Biafrans exploited this opportunity to liberate about 200 villages between Owerri and Port Harcourt. Offensive operations were also conducted in heavy bouts of rainfall; the Biafrans quickly learned that after the rain the Nigerians were generally preoccupied drying out their uniforms and tents.

Regardless of what tactics the Biafrans employed during the war they always had to face the harsh reality of the Nigerian total superiority in artillery and armour. When describing the fighting on the Northern Front in 1967 one student of the war said of the Biafran defensive and Nigerian offensive strategies;

> These only slowed the Federals, who used their superior firepower to saturate prepared positions and their mobility advantage to outflank Biafran strong points. At Obollo Eke, for example, artillery and mortar shelling began at 6 a.m. August 3, 1967, and continued until 8 a.m. After a brief attack, artillery preparations resumed, followed by another probe: This alternating pattern of two hours of shelling and a probing attack continued during daylight hours for four days before the Rebels were pushed out of Obollo Eke.'[12]

Chapter 3
Mercenaries in Biafra

After the relative success of European mercenaries fighting in Congo from 1960 to 1967 it was no surprise to see them involved in the Nigerian Civil War. In Congo large units of mercenaries had fought either with or without African troops at their side. A breakaway of the Congo's provinces of Katanga and South Kasai in 1960 saw the recruitment of a large number of Belgian and other European military experts into their armies and the Katangan leader Moise Tshombe used Belgian and French mercenaries to bolster his native troops during his attempted secession from DR Congo in 1960-1963. South Kasai's smaller Gendarmerie of 2,000 men also employed mercenaries but these were almost exclusively Belgians. Although South Kasai collapsed in 1961 and Katanga in 1963, the role of the mercenary in Africa was far from over. In a bizarre twist, the defeated Tshombe was invited to be Prime Minister of Congo by its President Kasavumba. The president desperately needed someone of his stature to deal with the new threat of Marxist led guerrillas called 'Simbas' or Lions who were threatening much of eastern Congo. With the Congolese Army or ANC of little use Tshombe looked to his former mercenaries from Katanga to help him fight the Simbas. As well as veterans of Congo hundreds of other mercenaries joined Tshombe serving in ten special 'Commandos' which acted as the strike force for the Congolese Army in 1964 – 67. Tshombe,

Colonel Rolf Steiner, the German commander of the 4th Commando Brigade, shows on his uniform his former career in the French Foreign Legion. Steiner had served with the Hitler Youth in 1945 and later joined the Foreign Legion serving in Indo-China for 7 years. The highest rank he reached in the Legion was sergeant and he proved to be great leader of small Biafran units. At his own admission he struggled when commanding the thousands of troops that made up the Brigade which was expanded to a Division. By late 1968 he was showing the strain of his command and Ojukwu expelled him from Biafra because of his 'erratic' behaviour.

having largely defeated the Simba's, had outlived his usefulness to the ANC by 1965 and its Commander in Chief, General Mobutu, overthrew him in November. Many mercenaries remained loyal to Tshombe and tried on two occasions to restore him to power by military means. The second mutiny of pro-Tshombe mercenaries took place in the summer of 1967 and its failure by November left a lot of unemployed mercenaries looking for further adventures in Africa.

The First Mercenary Units

The end of the fighting in Congo should probably have ended the 'Soldiers of Fortune' chapter in Africa. However, the outbreak of civil war in Nigeria gave some of them further opportunities to ply the only trade they knew. Officially, Colonel Ojukwu did not use mercenaries until the end of 1967 when he was becoming increasingly desperate. There were unsubstantiated reports that some French mercenaries were in the eastern region for five months before the creation of Biafra. If this is true they certainly kept a low profile as the Nigerians did not claim that they existed even in the heightened state of panic in 1967.

As the war situation worsened for the Biafrans, Ojukwu was advised to use some of the unemployed mercenaries hanging around in the bars of Africa and Europe to bolster his forces. He knew that employing any number of mercenaries would be expensive but saw them as a short-term measure. The plan was for a small force of mercenaries to train Biafran recruits rather than fight at the frontline. Ojukwu did not envisage sending units of mercenaries to act as a spearhead for his army but he hoped their presence would reassure his soldiers. In late 1967, the Frenchman Roger Faulques (former legionnaire of the French Foreign Legion) arrived in Biafra with 53 men – instead of the 100 he had promised – all his former

Three soldiers of the Biafran 4th Commando Division are seen at a checkpoint close to their headquarters. Two of the men are commandos and are distinguishable by the skull and crossbones patches on their shirt sleeves. Their comrade, who is part of the elite HQ Guard, has the letters CP for Command Post on his armband. Berets worn by the Biafran Army tended to be black although some members of the 4th Division wore theirs in the unit colour. (Author's Collection)

comrades from the DRC. They were to act purely as 'advisors' but while Faulques was away looking for arms, equipment and more recruits his men decided to take matters into their own hands. The arrogance of the mercenaries after their previous victories in Congo led a group of them to launch a frontal attack on Nigerian positions at the recently captured port of Calabar, armed only with Lanchester sub-machineguns. To their astonishment they ran into strong Nigerian positions and were forced to withdraw having suffered five casualties.

The official part of Faulques' mercenaries' mission got off to a poor start when they travelled towards Calabar in Land Rovers – with no scouts ahead of them. After coming under fire, they were forced to de-bus and continue on foot. However, due to the lack of reconnaissance, this operation ended in another fiasco: five men were killed, and the body of one of them, Henri Blocke, then paraded for the press. A 10% casualty rate was far too high for the mercenaries to take and nearly all of them decided to get out of Biafra after this experience.

When Falques returned from Paris he realised that the mission was hopeless and he told Ojukwu that he was leaving and taking his men with him. Explaining that his decision was due poor equipment and the fact they had been given bolt-on action rifles instead of sub-machineguns to which they were used, Falques managed to get away.

Colonel Steiner poses at the side of his personal Land Rover which is decorated with all the insignia of the 4th Commando Brigade in the summer of 1968. On the door of the vehicle is the white skull and crossbones insignia which is also featured on the flag at the front. The boy soldier who acts as Steiner's bodyguard has insignia of the French Foreign Legion paratrooper on his beret. It probably has been donated to the boy by Steiner himself who has the chest badge of the Legion's paratroopers on his breast. (Private Collection)

4th Commando Brigade

Neither Ojukwu's bad experiences with the first group of mercenaries, or the fact that recruitment of such troops was an expensive luxury for cash-starved Biafra, did not discourage him. After desperately looking around, he found other ways to utilise the large number of veterans from diverse wars around the continent. Eventually a group of individuals surfaced in Biafra, including a couple of US citizens; one called Nick Bishop (a 29-year-old who had served with Mike Hoare in DRC); and one reportedly named Major C. C. Watson, who was a claymore-mine expert.[1] In July 1967, even Mike Hoare turned up and was promptly tasked with raising a similar force to his former 5th Commando – this time for Ojukwu. However, Hoare saw enough to quickly conclude that Biafra was in a dire situation and could not be saved by a handful of mercenaries. Indeed, in December 1967, he went on the record to say:

> In my view the last thing that is required is the intervention of mercenary troops on either side, and I strongly advocate all those who might be thinking along these lines to drop the idea. Personally, I intend to take no part in it. I am totally convinced that such an intervention would aggravate the situation and lead to an alarming escalation, not excluding the possibility of the introduction of Cuban or Russian troops. The conflict must be kept down to size, local and African.[2]

When the first group of mercenaries left Biafra in early 1968 one man chose to stay behind because he wanted to continue to help the Biafran war effort. This enthusiastic mercenary was a 38-year-old German; ex-Legionnaire Rolf Steiner. Despite efforts by Falques to persuade Steiner to abandon the lost cause he insisted on staying. Over the next few weeks Steiner went on to prove himself in several small-scale skirmishes with the Nigerians, and was then approached by the Bifran GOC, Major Madeibo, with a request to form a commando unit of 100 men. The emerging company soon took part in a successful guerrilla action against the Nigerian Army at Enugu and was reinforced to 150-180.

Encouraged, Ojukwu then asked Steiner to realise his earlier idea for an elite unit of Biafrans that would be commanded by a small group of mercenaries. Initially at least, the German was not enthusiastic, but the Biafran leader persisted, promising Steiner he would get the pick of the officer cadets about to graduate from the Biafran War College and much of the new weaponry about to arrive in Biafra. Allocated 1,200 troops and a disused school, Steiner began training his unit with the help of a handful of mercenaries left in the territory.

The first of these was Giorgio Norbiatto, a 30-year-old who had served with the Italian marines in DRC: he was given command of the emerging 4th Commando Brigade's 'marine' unit. The second was Taffy Williams, of Welsh extraction born in South Africa, and a veteran of the secessionist war in Katanga. The third foreign mercenary was Louis 'Paddy' Maloney, a 54-year-old Irishman who had lived in Africa for 22 years. He became the principal mechanic of the brigade, responsible for keeping most of its vehicles and weaponry operational. Two other mercenaries that joined Steiner were Johnny Erasmus, a 25-year-old Rhodesian, and a Glaswegian called Alexander Ramsey Gay. Erasmus was an expert in explosives who had deserted from the Rhodesian Army and went on to build mines and other home-made weapons. Gay was a former bank clerk who had served with the famous Belgian mercenary Schramme in DRC in 1968. The last mercenary to join was a 33-year-old Corsican called Armand Ianarelli, who flew into Gabon to offer his services. According to Steiner, he wanted to fight for the sheer thrill of it all and went on to be one of the longest serving mercenaries.

In the first few months of its existence the brigade suffered its first mercenary fatality in early May when Norbiatto was killed in a 'one-man-stand', while covering the withdrawal of his unit. However, once the troops completed their training, and after being armed with weapons acquired from French sources in 1968, the unit soon began proving its worth in a series of raids behind enemy lines. From photographic and news sources it appears that Thompson sub-machineguns and bolt action Mausers were the main weapons used by the commandoes. The officers carried vz. 58s and FN/FALs, while Steiner was usually seen armed only with his Colt .45 automatic pistol. Heavier weaponry for the brigade, according to Steiner, included sixteen 81mm and twelve 60mm mortars. Steiner said at one point that he had thirty 81mm mortars as well as four 105mm field guns donated to the 4th by Ojukwu after he gave the Biafran leader 300 rifles.

The Biafran Fire Force

Before long, not only Ojukwu, but Steiner too, saw the 4th Commando Brigade as the 'fire force' of the Biafran armed forces: better trained and equipped than any other unit of the army, and commanded by officers Steiner was permitted to draft from the air force, navy and police (with Ojukwu's backing), once complete the brigade boasted about 5,000 men in total. Although suffering a relatively high casualty rate, it was constantly kept well-staffed, because there were enough volunteers willing to serve in an

The Corsican mercenary Armand Iaranelli and his second in command a French man called Boucher wait apprehensively in an ambush position with their men in 1968. Iaranelli and Boucher both carry FN/FAL rifles while his men have a variety of types of rifles and sub-machineguns. A well organised guerrilla war against the Nigerian Federal Army would have caused their long supply lines through Biafran territory to be fragile to say the least. (Author's Collection)

After the departure of Rolf Steiner from Biafra the number of mercenaries fighting for Ojukwu fell. One small group of less than half a dozen men stayed with the 4th Commando under the command of Taffy Williams. These three men come from two different countries with from left to right Armand Iaranelli from Corsica, a man called Boucher who was probably French and a Belgian Marc Goosens. (Author's Collection)

'elite unit'. Correspondingly, Steiner vastly expanded his training system: from the original three camps, he eventually established seven training schools (designated 1 – 7), each capable of training 200 troops. All run by foreign mercenaries, the schools taught the troops not only standard military skills, but also how to conserve ammunition.

While the first half of 1968 went well for the 4th Brigade, during the second half the unit was forced to fight as a conventional outfit. On Ojukwu's order, it became involved in the battles for Aba and Onitsha, where it lost thousands of troops in pointless frontal assaults on Nigerian positions. Pointless orders from above were not the only reason for the unit's poor performance: fighting in a conventional role exposed the commandos to the better-armed Nigerians. Unsurprisingly, by the end of this campaign, the 4th Commando Brigade was down to a mere 1,000 – out of 7,000 at the start. In total, it was estimated that the unit lost 8,400 men and boys in the first six months of its existence. Obviously, such a massive casualty rate was simply unsustainable.[3]

Aghast with the wasteful fashion in which their unit was deployed, Steiner and his men – who had deep respect for the bravery of the troops they had trained, and genuine regard for the Biafran case – complained.[4] The mercenaries were proud of what they had achieved with meagre resources and constantly attempted to improve the 4th Command Brigade, regardless of its catastrophic losses. Indeed, in early October 1968, Steiner travelled to Gabon with the intention of organising an amphibious operation against the Nigerian Navy. When this plan fell through he instead recruited 12 mercenaries from the bars of the Gabonese capital Libreville and returned to Biafra. With their help, the brigade was expanded into a division and its strength was increased to 10,000 men – at least in theory. In practice, the survivors of the original brigade were reinforced through the addition of troops from the 8th and 12th brigades. However, not only the latter two units but also new recruits lacked weaponry. When one journalist asked him a question on this topic, Steiner frankly replied: 'I command 8,500 men but only have 1,000 rifles for 10,000 men' – and how he was forced to ambush the Nigerians in order to seize their weapons. Nevertheless, he remained determined:

'We only have one choice, to defend ourselves or die. They don't take prisoners so nor do we.' [5]

This close up of the Flemish mercenary Marc Goosens was taken either by a visiting journalist or by a fellow soldier of fortune. Goosens was interviewed shortly before his death in battle and he talked about his motivation for helping the Biafrans. Another source says that Goosens hated the British and fought for Biafra partly because they were supporting the Nigerians. He had previously fought on the Royalist side in the long running civil war in the Yemen along with a number of other mercenaries. (Author's Collection)

A group of European mercenaries fighting for the Biafrans gather around a map before going into action in November 1968. They have been given the ominous task of liberating the city of Onitsha from the Nigerian Army. The photographer who may well have been a fellow mercenary has written the names of the men around the edge of the photograph. They are from bottom left clockwise: the Welshman, Taffy Williams, the Belgian Marc Goosens, the 350lbs Frenchman 'Tiny Bill' Billois, an unknown mercenary called Boucher and the Corsican Armand Iaranelli. (Author's Collection)

Three of the dwindling number of mercenaries fighting for the Biafrans look at a map before launching an assault. They are checking the positions of the Nigerian defences around the city of Onitsha in November 1968. The man in the centre with the steel helmet is Taffy Williams a South African of Welsh decent. On his left sucking on a straw is Coriscan Armand Ianarelli and to his right the Belgian Marc Goosens. Goosens was given the job of leading the commandos into battle and they were soon to come under heavy fire. The Belgian was hit by a bullet and died immediately and his faithful men had to carry his bulky body back to Biafran lines. (Author's Collection)

With the favourable treatment that he was supposed to receive from Ojukwu the lack of arms was becoming a real issue for Steiner. Moreover, his mental health was affected by the constant responsibility for both his mercenaries and his troops: after all, the German was originally only a sergeant-major by qualification, despite his illustrious new rank of a full colonel.

Steiner's Expulsion

By early November 1968, Steiner was not only feeling the pressure of his command, but his good relationship with Ojukwu was in tatters. Reportedly, he distanced himself from the command and ignored several instructions from the Biafran leader. With tensions developing between the two men, something had to give. What happened next remains disputed to the present day.

In his autobiography, Steiner wrote that there was a dispute over Ojukwu demanding a punishment for a group of mercenaries that had humiliated the Biafran leader's uncle while underway to Uli Airport to get fuel for their vehicles. Steiner put them under a house-arrest, but the furious Ojukwu demanded much worse. Other sources stress that Steiner's men had stolen vehicles from the Swedish Red Cross to use as military staff transport, while the third version said that Steiner struck a Biafran officer who had stolen arms for the 4th Commando Division.

Whatever the reason was, the German was summoned to the

Goosens' lifeless body is carried back across a stream after his death early in the Biafran attack on the defences of Onitsha. Some of his men stole the money that Goosens had in his pockets and were nearly killed by their commander Taffy Williams. In their eyes the soldiers probably meant no disrespect to Goosens and simply thought he no longer needed it! (Albert Grandolini Collection)

State House, and drove there together with four mercenaries. In the course of the following meeting of all Biafran divisional commanders, Ojukwu demanded Steiner be removed from his command. Realising that most of his nominal colleagues were actively campaigning for his removal, and in an increasingly charged atmosphere, Steiner felt he no longer had the trust and confidence of the Biafran leader. He handed him his resignation letter, which Ojukwu – reluctantly – accepted. The two men parted on good terms and the German went to re-join his men downstairs. However, on the way out, he was told he would have to undergo a search. The German refused to hand over his pistol to the Biafran guards, causing a scuffle in which Steiner hit one of the opponents before he and his men were overpowered and bundled into several Land Rovers. Instead of being executed on the spot, as some of the Biafran officers demanded, he was escorted to the airport and along with his entourage was flown out to nearby Gabon. After the departure of Rolf Steiner and some of his men, a small group of mercenaries, including Taffy Williams, was still determined to fight for Biafra. These included Belgian Marc Goosens who had served in the Yemen in the mid-1960s, and was motivated to fight for Biafra partly by his dislike of the British Government.

The Last Battle of the Mercenaries

The brigade that Steiner left behind had been recently organised into three separate 'strike forces', or battalions, each about 1,000 strong. The first was named the 'Ahoada' Strike Force and was commanded by Armand Ianarelli; the second, the 'Abaliki' Strike Force, was under Erasmus. Although not officially the elite force, the 'Guards Strike Force' was led by Taffy Williams with Alexander Gay as his deputy commander. This was the composition with which this mercenary-commanded outfit was to see its last action in November 1968. At the time, it was ordered into an ill-fated attempt to re-take Onitsha by a frontal attack on well-prepared Nigerian defences. The result was predictable: in presence of a French news crew, about 4,000 troops ran into a hail of bullets, at least two of which struck and killed Goosens. Another 'casualty' of this attack was Ianarelli, who was bitten by a snake as he moved through the bush. The attack was repeated on the next day, but ended in the same fashion, and ultimately only served as an illustration for how misjudged the Biafran tactics were by this time – perhaps also how desperate its military commanders were to prove the worth of this precious unit to Ojukwu. Immediately afterwards, most of the mercenaries decided to get out of the territory – while they still could.[6]

Mercenaries After 1968

After the catastrophe of November 1968, only nine mercenaries remained in Biafra. They were distributed around the territory, each setting up their own small units. Five had left the country before long, followed by an unknown Englishman, leaving only three to continue: Ianarelli, Williams and Gay spent the rest of the year working as training officers only, until leaving in early 1969.

Another, rather farcical mercenary involvement in Biafra saw the appearance of a 15-strong force led Capitan Maurice Lucien-Brun, supposed to run a 'guerrilla war' behind Nigerian lines. This scheme was abandoned before its implementation. Thus, the Biafran Army was forced to fight the final year of its existence entirely on its own.

Other Mercenaries and Advisers

There were other names that appeared in the press during the war as potential mercenaries and volunteers for Biafra: indeed, early during the war, there was no end of false rumours about the presence and identity of these 'soldiers of fortune'. Probably the most exotic was the so-called 'Black Eagle'; Colonel Hubert Julian, a black American pilot. He had flown for the Ethiopians in their war with Italy in 1935-1936 where he also proved to be a skilled self-publicist. The famous Belgian mercenary Colonel Jean Schramme was also mentioned as being in Biafra. Like many other rumours that flew around during the two and a half years of fighting this proved to be a false report.

In early October 1967, Nigerian press reports claimed that 20 'Asians' were amongst the mercenaries killed during the ill-fated attack on the city of Calabar. In February 1968, press reports claimed that 50 'Chinese mercenaries' had been killed in fighting in the Onitsha sector and – later the same month – that 23 'white mercenaries' had been killed in the Calabar sector. In October 1967, there were reports that Colonel Ojukwu had executed five white mercenaries for disobeying their orders. Finally, in 1968, the Nigerians claimed that citizens of Portugal, Gabon, Tanzania, France, Rhodesia, and China were fighting for the Biafrans.

Indeed, the mix of mercenaries that worked with the Biafrans

This rather grainy photograph is of Michel, a little known French mercenary who was the cousin of 'Tiny Bill' Billois. He appears to have arrived in Biafra with Billois and was said to never leave his more experienced cousin's side. He was described as a totally insignificant member of the mercenary group who "made no impression both before and after he left Biafra". (Author's Collection)

was quite eclectic and included a number of adventurers. In addition to Steiner and Taffy Williams, these included Commandant Kochanowsky, a 50-year-old Pole who had fought with the British Army in northern Africa before joining the Foreign Legion in France. Reportedly, he took no pay for his service and fought for the Biafrans for three months before leaving mysteriously. Another man with a rather unsavoury reputation was an Englishman, Steve Neeley, who Frederick Forsyth described in his book *The Outsider* as, 'unpleasant.' He drove around in a Land Rover decorated with the skull of a Nigerian soldier he had killed. Neeley died in the Abakakaliki sector in a fire fight[7]

In the rather shady world of the mercenary activities in Africa of the 1960s, sometimes only the first name of the individual was known. This was the case with 'Captain Alec', a former British paratrooper who served in Biafra.

There were a number of 'advisors' who were listed as having served the Biafrans during the civil war. These included 'White Johnny' Juan Correa, a 37-year-old Puerto Rican and veteran of the Korean War. His task during the war was the disposal of unexploded bombs that had been dropped by the Nigerian Air Force, and to train the Biafrans in that art – thus also obtaining explosives for homemade weapons produced by the RAP. His team of bomb disposers would travel to anywhere that had suffered an air raid and harvest their potentially deadly dud bombs. According to Correa, many of the bombs deployed by the Nigerian Air Force dated back to the 1940s, while some were little more than modified fire-extinguishers, filled with dynamite.[8]

Secret Involvement in Biafra

Until recently it has always been accepted that we knew the full extent of mercenary involvement in Biafra from 1967 until 1970. There had been reports in the Nigerian press in December 1967 that there was a force of 150 South Africans fighting for the Biafrans. This report was entirely false at the time but 18 months later there was a South African involvement in Biafra but of just a five-man force not 150. South African journalist Al J Venter who was in Biafra during the war reveals the truth in his 2015 book, *Biafra's War 1967 – 1970*. Venter interviewed the leader of a small South African force of military advisors that spent six months in 1969 training Biafran troops. Major Jan Breytenbach, the founder of the South African Special Forces in the 1970s, cut his teeth commanding this 'mercenary' group. The scheme had been suggested by the pro-Biafran French and it soon got official, but secret, sanction from the South African defence minister, PW Botha. As far as the South Africans were concerned if helping the Biafrans caused problems for the Nigerians that was fine by them. South Africa was isolated by the majority of the world's governments due its apartheid policy. The Organisation of African Unity (OAU) was behind Nigeria and anything that disputed the most populous country in Africa was to be encouraged. The plan in early 1969 was for a small handpicked group of South Africans to train a Biafran special forces unit under a 6-month contract. Breytenbach was allowed to recruit three other South African military specialists, including a radio operator. They flew into Biafra and after meeting Colonel Ojukwu they were provided with a training camp and 500 volunteers. The four South Africans insisted on being issued with the FN/FAL that they were used to instead of the inferior weapons offered by the Biafrans; the Biafrans were issued with MAS-36 rifles and Thompson sub-machineguns which were the only available weapons for them. It was soon discovered that most of the Biafrans were unfit for service and many, after eating a substandard diet for two years, did not have the required physique. The South Africans soon whittled them down to 100 of the most suitable candidates and began their training. Because of the dire war situation, the intensive training was broken down into a truncated month-long course. Immediately after they finished training the Biafran special forces were ordered by a desperate Ojukwu to go on their first behind-the-lines operations. They penetrated Federal lines in the vicinity of Port Harcourt and attacked Nigerian units in a series of 'hit and run' raids. Although it was important to keep the South African presence in Biafra secret the advisors decided to go beyond their remit and fight with their men. Several of the South Africans, including Breytenbach, were wounded during the raids and they soon realised that the odds were too high for the Biafrans to overcome. When their contracts were up none of the men wanted to renew them and they were flown out of the country in late 1969. Major Breytenbach also revealed to Venter an audacious plan involving the use of a South African submarine. The plan was that the submarine would attack Soviet freighters bringing in supplies to the southern Nigerian ports. Planning for the scheme was well underway and according to sources it was only cancelled at the last minute, presumably to avoid international outcry.

Venter also reported that one of the most 'colourful' mercenaries of the 1960s also had a little-known role in Biafra. The Frenchman Colonel Bob Denard had served in Katanga in the early 1960s and then spent a short period in the Middle East. He was advising the Yemeni Royalists in their war with the Republicans until 1963. Afterwards he returned to Africa and the Congo where he joined the fight against the communist Simbas in the mid-1960s. He served as an officer in the mercenary force which was supporting the Congolese Government Army before ending up in command of the 6th Commando, which spent 1964 and 1965 spearheading the military campaign. His employer, Tshombe, was overthrown by the Congolese Army commander General Mobutu in 1966: Denard refused to obey his orders and took some of his men to the east of the Congo. There he helped organise a mercenary revolt in support of Tshombe in the summer of 1967 but was wounded and left the Congo. Still looking for employment, Denard was reported to have travelled to Biafra and met Ojukwu. Officially, he soon decided the odds were too high for him and the men he had brought to fight. According to Venter, however, he and his men stayed in Biafra and worked undercover training the army, well away from the visiting newsmen. Their departure from Biafra had been a ruse played out at the insistence of the French who did not want their presence to be made public. The number of men he brought with him is not known but it cannot be as high as the 100 mercenaries frequently quoted in the contemporary press.

Chapter 4
Weaponry of the Biafran Army

From the early stages of the civil war it became apparent that Biafra was a 'David' in comparison to Nigeria's 'Goliath' – in both number of troops and quantity of weapons. Colonel Ojukwu's proud boasts of 1966 and 1967 that he had plenty of arms to defend Biafra with, were hollow words. Frederick Forsyth noted that the Biafrans were in a desperate situation:

> Manpower apart, Ojukwu had an almost complete lack of weaponry. There was no artillery, no armour, no support weapons, no signal equipment and few battalion transport vehicles. In infantry weapons he had some newly imported sub-machineguns, the old Police Authority bolt-action rifles and masses of shotguns.[1]

With too few rifles and hardly any machineguns, mortars or artillery pieces the Biafran Army was at a severe disadvantage. Even when the level of arms increased from late 1968 the Biafrans never got anywhere near the amount of armaments that the Federal Army had. The lack of a reliable arms supply meant that armaments had to be bought from any available source. This meant that gullible Biafran agents were often sold poor quality, damaged and out-of-date arms by unscrupulous dealers. Arms arrived in Biafra in job lots with sometimes packing cases full of rifles and other small arms that were unlabelled. It was also the case that munitions' officers would unpack a batch of rifles or machineguns with no instructions on how to assemble and maintain them or even their calibre.

Financing the War

The Biafran War effort, and especially the purchase of armaments, were financed by a number of sources. Ojukwu used much of his personal fortune to buy arms before the war, claiming he had spent £1 million in total. In the last few months before the east seceded, Ojukwu and his local government managed to salt away an estimated $6 million. Of course, when the war began the eastern administration had millions in Nigerian currency which was still legal tender in Biafra. Biafran officials were aware that the Nigerian government could change its currency at any time, making the money held by Biafra worthless: this was the principal reason for the Biafran rush to buy arms during the first weeks of the war. When the Nigerians did change their currency in January 1968 the Biafrans issued their own currency, but it had no value on the international market and as the Nigerian currency was being changed, the Biafrans were trying to offload the money they had before it became worthless. In a series of often fruitless attempts to sell their Nigerian currency at the last minute the Biafrans were reported to have lost a staggering £30 million. In an attempt to raise funds, the Biafran Government issued a number of 'secured' bonds during the war.

After the war, the Biafrans acknowledged that a large amount of foreign currency that they had came from a highly controversial source. By 1968 thousands of Biafran civilians, and especially

A typical Biafran infantry unit poses for the camera in their jungle base with most of its men armed with Mauser rifles. The Mauser 98k was an out of date weapon but its was favoured by many in the Biafran Army because it did not waste precious ammunition. It was reported that most of these came from French sources taken from stores of old German Mausers. Some of the men have put cloth plugs in the end of their gun barrels to stop the humid atmosphere damaging them. (Albert Grandolini Collection)

This young Biafran soldier waits to go into action armed with the Czechoslovakian made vz. 58 assault rifle in 1968. Quite large numbers of the vz. 58 which is often wrongly described as a British 'Madison' rifle were imported by Biafra before the conflict. Although the soldier had managed to acquire a military field cap his patterned shirt shows that many Biafrans went into action in civilian clothes. (Private Collection)

This well turned out guard waits outside the Biafran Army headquarters for the arrival of His Excellency Colonel Ojukwu in the summer of 1968. At this stage in the civil war few Biafran troops would have been as well uniformed or armed as their army struggled to survive. Four of the guard are armed with the vz. 58 while at least one other has a captured Federal BM-59 imported from Italy before the outbreak of the war. (Author's Collection)

children, were dying from starvation every day. Therefore, the Biafran government began charging the Red Cross and other relief agencies a landing fee when they flew in food for their own people. This policy was of course highly criticised at the time although some commentators have excused it. The justification for the charges meted out to the relief agencies was that the Biafrans were fighting for their survival. Although they appreciated the help given by the various agencies, some said they would rather have been given a rifle to defend themselves with than a bag of millet. With money so tight for the Biafrans, they began to produce estimates of how much each battle or operation would cost them. The best-known examples of such calculations were the defences of the towns of Aba and Owerri in 1968: each had cost £100,000 spent on the arms and ammunition expended.

Early Arms Shipments 1966-1967

In 1966, an arms shipment of between 960 and 1,000 Lanchster M1938 sub-machineguns was lost in the swamps of Cameroon following an air crash. These rather archaic looking weapons had not seen service with the British Army but had been issued to Royal Navy landing parties. Although the vast majority were lost in the swamps some somehow found their way into Biafran hands and a few were issued to the first group of European mercenaries in 1967. Faced with numerous setbacks Ojukwu and his agents did not give up their search for suitable armament. In February 1967 – a full four months before the secession – the first substantial arms shipments arrived secretly in eastern Nigeria. Reportedly organised by the mysterious Belgian arms dealer Baron Christian von Oppenheim, and worth £541,477, the first included 20 heavy machineguns, 40 light machineguns, 195 sub-machineguns, 408 automatic assault rifles, 355 semi-automatic rifles, 1,240 Lee-Enfield MK.IV rifles, and 25 pistols. The second delivery, in late March 1967, included 206 automatic assault rifles, 210 semi-automatics, 240 MK.IVs and 125 pistols. On 6 April 1967, a third consignment arrived, including 13 light machineguns, 45 sub-machineguns, 49 automatic rifles, 255 semi-automatic rifles, and 380 MK IVs. The final arms delivery from this source arrived on 13 April 1967 and consisted of 2 light machineguns, 60 sub-machineguns and 60 automatic rifles. All of the arms were stored safely in several locations, with some being kept in Ojukwu's Governor's Residence. The Colonel obviously wanted to keep an eye on the arms for which he claimed to have spent £1 million of his personal fortune.

Arms Shipments 1967-1968

Once fighting began, in July 1967, the need for more arms and ammunition became critical for Biafra. Agents who were trying to buy arms from the international arms market were constantly duped by unscrupulous dealers. The bigger private arms dealers, who played by the rules, could get the necessary 'end user licences' to sell arms to Biafra. One of the biggest arms dealers, the American Sam Cummings maintained that although politely approached by Biafran agents after 1967 he always equally politely declined. Dealers like Cummings would approach the world's governments and offer to buy up surplus or out of date arms from their stores. His reputation for fair dealing, he insisted in his autobiography written in 1984, was more important than the money he could have made from the desperate Biafrans. Other less wary dealers could usually get hold of job lots left in stores, often since the end of the Second World War. These were often leftovers that the bigger and more scrupulous arms dealers had rejected in the past. They would then sell the rifles and other small arms to the Biafrans, often without the correct ammunition. Rifles also arrived damaged, worn, and with no cleaning kits and pull-throughs. Tools like these were essential to maintain the rifles in good condition, especially in the tropical conditions of West Africa. Larger weapons like mortars and the odd piece of artillery would arrive rusty and missing parts like rangefinders. The poor condition of the weapons often made them dangerous to use and there are numerous reports of deaths caused by faulty arms in the Biafran Army. Because of the desperation to buy arms the Biafran agents were ripe for exploitation by the less scrupulous arms dealers they dealt with. When decent arms and equipment were available to buy in Europe the prices suddenly multiplied when Biafran officials appeared. For example, in a 6-month period the price of the average rifle on the arms market doubled. Some dealers used the opportunity to offload old, damaged and unsuitable rifles and other arms to the Biafrans. While some stories of dodgy arms deals sound too bizarre to be true many have been verified by eyewitnesses. For example, the Biafrans were desperate to build a viable navy to counter the Federal navy's blockade of its southern ports. Reportedly, one official paid £145,000 for three ex-Royal Navy torpedo boats which had been sold off as surplus for £10,000 a few years before. Other exotic stories of mis-selling and sheer criminal behaviour by arms dealers including one about a dummy torpedo. This was supposed to have been bought by the Biafrans to sink the Federal navy's flagship NNS *Nigeria*. It was reported to have been built by a film prop company when the arms dealer could not find a real one on the market. The bill for the torpedo was £2,000 and when built it was offered to the Biafrans at a reported £100,000, although even in their desperation it is doubtful that they bought it. Another scheme to sink the ship involved the building of a remote-controlled craft which was to be filled with napalm. The price for the 50,000 pounds of explosives that were needed, as well as well as the hire of the experts needed, was quoted by the Englishman who suggested the scheme at £450,000. Some agents did not even go as far as creating false arms-deals with one Central European buyer given £75,000 to buy arms for Biafra and then disappearing with the money. Other arms shipments may have looked legitimate, but the contents of the crates may not have been as useful as first thought. In July, a US-registered Riley Dove light transport aircraft flew into Port Harcourt airport from Switzerland. It was carrying a load of 2,000 Hungarian-manufactured rifles which were reported to be hunting guns. Although the weapons may well have all been shotguns, it was reported that the Hungarian government wanted to offload a lot of 'Levant' sports rifles. These were a small calibre single shot training rifle which had been issued to the Hungarian Fascist Youth Movement in the Second World War. They were later issued to the Communist Youth organisations after 1945 but were surplus to requirements by the 1960s. While useful for training recruits, the Levant rifles would have been of little use to soldiers in combat. The problem for the Biafrans was that most of their arms agents could not distinguish one rifle from another and were also unable in the early days to judge how useful the weapons they were buying were to the Biafran Army.

Hungry Biafran militiamen scramble for their rations during a break in fighting while clutching onto their firearms. They are typical of the types of irregulars and militia that had to face the regular Federal Army in the early stages of the war. By 1968 when this photograph was taken the regular army could issue most of its men with a Mauser rifle at least. Most of these men are armed with double barrelled shotguns which would only have been of use in close quarter fighting. The Biafrans were pleased to be issued with any kind of firearm even when little or no ammunition was available for their weapons. (Romano Cagnoni)

After finishing their three week training course these army recruits are taking weapons from a pile of newly arrived rifles on their parade ground in June 1969. Many of the weapons supplied to the Biafrans from 1968 were bolt action rifles and most of the rifles here are ex-German Army Mauser 98ks. Amongst the Mausers are a few British Lee Enfields and some Czech vz. 52s which had been delivered in 1967.

Light machinegun crews line up for inspection at Elele, 30 miles south of Owerri on the Port Harcourt road in 1968. This well armed unit is armed mainly with the well known German MG34 light machineguns which saw widespread service with the Biafrans. The man second from left is the exception and is equipped with a Czechoslovakian Model 52 light machinegun in its belt fed version. Some of the men are wearing what appears to be the Biafran made version of the construction helmet which were made out of milk tins. (Private Collection)

Captured Armament

Because of the lack of reliable supplies of rifles and other small arms the capture of modern weapons from the Federal army was vital. Every skirmish or battle was seen a potential source of weapons and equipment and during the first year of the war just about kept the army going. While news reports usually mentioned any materials taken by either side after a battle, the best way to judge the flow of arms from Federal sources is to study photographs of the war. What is obvious is that any FN/FALS, G3s or other modern rifles were claimed by officers and NCOs. The rest of the troops were armed with the remains of the Czech arms delivered in 1966 or early 1967, or with the odd Lee Enfield. The idea that every type of weapon available

A young Biafran machinegunner aims his ex-British Army Bren .303 light machinegun towards enemy lines from the shelter of the rain forest. Only a handful of Bren Guns were still in armouries in Eastern Nigeria when the region seceded in May 1967. Additional Bren's were captured from the Nigerian Federal Army who used theirs in the early months of the civil war. (Romano Cagnoni)

With a look of apprehension and terror on his face this Biafran soldier moves through the jungle armed with a Czechoslovakian made P27 'Pancerovka' anti-tank grenade launcher loaded and ready. The Pancerovka which could penetrate up to 250mm of armour was supplied in limited numbers to the Biafrans but as with most other weaponry re-supply of ammunition was always a problem. (Romano Cagnoni)

on the arms market found its way to Biafra is a myth. When looking at the arms carried by an average Biafran unit before mid-1968 it is surprising to see the same types appearing again and again. Regardless of the number of different types of rifle and sub-machinegun in service, the job of a Biafran logistics officer was tough to say the least. From 1967, until more regular arms shipments arrived in 1968, any captured weaponry was like 'gold dust' to the Biafrans. Biafran units would use any measure they could to get Nigerian arms, although perhaps surprisingly there is no record of corrupt Federal officers selling arms or ammunition to the enemy. The proof of the desperation of the Biafrans to obtain arms and ammunition was shown by an incident in the fighting for Onitsha in 1968. During Nigerian river assaults on the city in April 1968 the Biafrans on the opposite bank changed their tactics. They had noticed in previous attacks that much of the weaponry and equipment carried by the killed and injured Nigerian troops ended up at the bottom of the river. So instead of firing at them mid-stream they took a risk and waited until they were in the shallows or even let them come ashore before opening fire so they could retrieve the rifles and other weaponry from the dead Nigerians. [2]

The Biafran crew of a rare piece of ordinance prepare to fire their British 4.2 inch MK2 mortar towards Nigerian positions. Most mortars in Biafran service were the Second World War vintage British Army 3-inch or 2-inch models. Before the Biafrans launched an operation they would spend several weeks squirreling away enough mortar bombs to fire a few towards Nigerian positions. Unfortunately, one round from a Biafran mortar could be answered by dozens from the Federal Army's positions. (Romano Cagnoni)

'Operation Mabel': French Arms Shipments of 1968-1970

In the summer of 1968, just as the struggling Biafrans were about to collapse after a series of military defeats, they received some vital support from France. A secret airlift, codenamed Operation Mabel, was organised with the agreement of a French Government which had mixed motives. Genuine sympathy for the plight of Biafra was mixed with President De Gaulle's wish to rival the British for influence in West Africa in the 1960s. It was directed by Jacques Foccart, with the assistance of the French Secret Service, and the wholehearted support of President De Gaulle. Jacques Foccart was one of the most influential French officials in the De Gaulle government and had the official title of Secretary General for African Affairs. His role was to operate a close relationship between France and the leaders of their former African colonies; like Gabon, Ivory Coast, Togo and Dahomey. On 1 August the French had made a public declaration in support of Biafran self-determination. Without ever officially recognising Biafra, the French were to give them enough material support to keep their war effort going. A priority for the Biafrans was to get arms from the French; especially anti-tank weapons. The first large shipments of French small arms began to arrive by air in Biafra in October 1968. All of the early deliveries came via the ex-French colonial, West African states of Gabon and the Ivory Coast. Both nations' small armies were reported to have been asked by the French to send their old weapons to Biafra. These arms would then be 'officially' replaced by more modern French rifles and other weaponry. Boxes of ammunition from the Ivory Coast were photographed by journalists on arrival in Biafra. Rifles seen in service with the Biafran Army after 1968 included the French MAS-36 which presumably came from this source. A large number of German Mausers of Second World War vintage probably came from French stores. They, like most Allied nations, stockpiled ex-German weapons for future use and some that arrived in Biafra appeared to be in mint condition having been captured from German factories in 1945. Another rifle seen amongst the 1968 shipments were a number of 1930s era Italian Carcano TS carbines. Smaller shipments of French and other arms had been arriving since September with a reported 30 – 40 tons arriving every night. Throughout late 1968 and into 1969 there was a steady stream of arms to Biafra, with 75 tons arriving over an 11-day period in mid-1969. In October 1969, 200 tonnes of arms were being flown into the rebel enclave per week which was just about enough to keep the Biafran army fighting. When questioned about the supply of French arms to Biafra, a high ranking French official admitted that he thought that the arsenals of Gabon and the Ivory Coast must be "somewhat low". Not all Biafran officials were happy with the military supplies sent to them by France especially as the quantities were never enough to win the war, only to prolong it. The Biafran Army Chief of Staff, Major-General Philip Effiong was particularly scathing. He said that the French military aid had only given more reasons for the suppliers of Nigerian arms, like the UK, to send larger amounts of munitions to balance things out. Effiong was quoted after the war as saying 'The bastards did more harm than good by raising false hopes and by providing the British with an excuse to reinforce Nigeria.'

Many Biafran officers were aware that the new arms, although welcome, were kept at a level that while encouraging them to continue to resist could not bring them victory. One well informed

In August 1968 the Biafran Army as part of an attempt to boost sagging morale put on display a variety of captured weaponry. The weapons included several of these 105mm pack howitzers from Italy which according to the placard were captured in fighting for Port Harcourt. Losing these guns would have been a blow for the Nigerian 3rd Marine Division fighting in that sector as they had only recently received artillery and armoured vehicles. (Author's Collection)

Another of the captured 105mm pack howitzers is put on display. This example lost its wheels when it was taken from the Nigerians. Capturing Federal Army weaponry in a usable condition was a constant problem for the Biafrans. The ingenuity of the RAP – 'Science Group' or even local blacksmiths would be tested to rig up new wheels so that the gun could be used. (Author's Collection)

source said that in total during 1968 the French gave the Biafrans £2,000,000 in arms and other military assistance. Estimates of the total value of the French military aid delivered before the war ended in January 1970 were put at £5,000,000.

Other Sources of Arms

Apart from a handful of small-calibre anti-aircraft guns and shells for the few field guns that Biafra possessed the majority of the arms shipments were small arms. These arms were made up mainly of out of date British, French, Soviet and Czech weapons. In August 1966, Ojukwu's agents were reported to have travelled to Israel asking the embattled state for arms. The persecution and massacres of the easterners led to some commentators calling them the 'Jews of Africa.' It was hoped that the Israelis would feel some empathy for the Ibos but as far as is known no arms were sold to the easterners. Other attempts were made by the newly seceded Biafra, but their appeals appear to have fallen on deaf ears. It was, however, reported by the Paris Bureau of the Associated Press news agency in July 1969 that the Biafrans were purchasing war material of Israeli origin from a 'third party.' This war material may well have been the older Arab small arms captured by the Israelis during the Six Day War of 1967. According to one US diplomatic source the "greatest service" that the Israelis performed for the Biafrans was in putting them in touch with the agents who were selling these captured weapons on their behalf. South Africa was also reported to be shipping between 25 and 50 tons of arms to Biafra per week. It was claimed that the majority of these shipments were made up of .303" ammunition for the Biafran rifles and machineguns of British origin.

Ammunition Shortages

When the Biafrans did receive small arms and other weaponry the next problem was keeping the weapons supplied with suitable ammunition. The Biafran Army suffered from an almost constant shortage of all kinds of ammunition throughout the war. A much-quoted figure for the number of bullets issued to Biafran soldiers was 1 round when on the defensive, 2 when on the offensive, and a really lucky soldier would get about 5 bullets at the start of an operation. The disparity in quantities of ammunition available between the two combatants is illustrated by a statistic from November 1968. This showed that the Nigerian Federal Army used 120 tons of ammunition that month in battle while the Biafran Army used 5 tons. The Shortage of ammunition was a constant constraint on Biafran operations and numerous attacks had to be called off when a unit simply ran out of bullets. On many occasions the Nigerians would try to goad the Biafrans into using up scarce bullets and then force them to withdraw when they ran out. When an operation was imminent the Biafran supply officers would go around literally begging, borrowing or stealing any small arms ammunition they could. The commanding officer and his ADC would even drive all the way to the nearest headquarters and come away with one box of ammunition if they were lucky. There were often an average of 3 shells per field gun and 20 bullets per rifle held at brigade level. This paltry reserve of ammunition was handed out to battalions on a day-by-day basis and depending on the level of military activity in their sectors. Even though the Biafran soldiers were well aware of the shortage of ammunition they sometimes could not control themselves. As late as 1969 Biafran soldiers were showing off for the news cameramen by firing off some of their precious ammunition into the air. Michael Leapman, on an operation with a platoon of 20 men in 1969, noted that as the unit advanced they sprayed the surrounding bush with bullets. He pointed out that the acute shortage of ammunition was not being made any easier by this practice. The company officer replied "I know but it is the only way that the men will advance. They are frightened by the noise and they are afraid that there may be Nigerians hiding in the undergrowth."[3] The shortage of small arms ammunition was made worse by the fact that the Nigerians fired off their bullets in unbelievable numbers. The usual quota for a single Nigerian machinegunner during a skirmish with the enemy would be at least three boxes. In contrast a whole Biafran brigade would be fortunate to have the same amount of ammunition. When advancing the Nigerians would simply spray the bush ahead of them with copious amounts of ammunition which literally shredded the leaves from the trees in their path. Efforts were made by Biafran armourers to adapt captured ammunition for the rifles and machineguns in their units. Bullets that didn't fit Biafran guns were crudely resized using old rifles as resizing dies by forcing the bullet into the chamber. The explosive powder had been removed from the cartridge beforehand and once they had been resized it was replaced and the bullet was glued. Needless to say, a number of the crudely made cartridges exploded injuring or killing the firer. Artillery shells were also in short supply with one Biafran battalion commander saying that when his field gun fired two rounds at the Nigerian positions they immediately replied with 90.[4] Another, probably exaggerating battalion commander went even further saying that for every shell that his artillery fired the Federals replied with 1,000 in return.[5] Biafran commanders were, not surprisingly, obsessed with hoarding as many shells as they could in preparation for operations. As one artillery officer complained, his unit did not usually have enough shells available to even 'warm up the barrel.' It was said that Biafran artillery officers counted the number of shells they fired individually; their Nigerian counterparts were said to count the amount of shells they used by the number of hours they were firing for.

This Nigerian Oerlikon 20mm anti-aircraft gun was captured during fighting at Bori and is on display to the press. War booty anti-aircraft guns were often transported to the Biafran main air field at Uli to try and protect it from Nigerian Air Force attacks. (Author's Collection)

Victorious Biafran troops help lift a captured Nigerian 40mm Bofors anti-aircraft gun from the lake at recently liberated Oguta in September 1968. Before they fled the Federal troops had pushed the gun and an armoured car into the lake but they did not destroy the cranes at the lakeside town. Both pieces of heavy weaponry were put into immediate service with the Biafran Army with the armoured car being named 'Oguta Boy'. (Private Collection)

A Biafran armoured lorry destroyed at Ore during the abortive invasion of the Mid-West by the Biafrans in 1967. This model of armoured vehicle has an improvised armoured box shaped cover on a standard truck chassis with a turret added to the top of the superstructure. Just visible here is the casing of the recoilless rifle round that put the vehicle out of action. Although not visible here, one or two machineguns would be fitted inside the turret but these did not protect it from the Nigerian recoilless rifle. (Author's Collection)

One of the Biafrans 'feared' Red Devil armoured vehicles lies on a road outside the city of Nsukku after an abortive attempt to re-capture it. The former Bren Gun Carriers were bought from the scrap yards of Europe and brought into Biafra before the war began. A heavy metal plate superstructure was added to the vehicles which made them not only 'top heavy' but also too heavy for their worn out engines to cope with. This meant they overheated after a short time in action leaving them as sitting ducks for the Nigerian recoilless rifles and artillery. (Private Collection)

The general shortage of ammunition was sometimes used as a convenient excuse for officers to withdraw from an engagement. If an officer did not want his unit to take part in an offensive he could claim that he had no bullets to give his troops. On a number of occasions, the arrival of a Land Rover or other HQ vehicle with a few boxes of ammunition would scupper their plans. At other times the excuse was genuine with commanders not having the minimum two 'offensive' rounds of ammunition to issue to their men. The shortage of ammunition on the Biafran side often led to risks being taken to fill the gaps. For instance, a delivery of 60mm mortar bombs were found when delivered to be smoke bombs. RAP scientists tried to adapt the bombs by replacing the chemicals with explosives but on at least four occasions they blew-up the mortar tubes killing their crews.

Being a logistics officer in the Biafran army must have been one of the most difficult jobs during the war, trying to meet all the demands being put on them. It was reported that one of the major problems in the Biafran military was the high suicide rate amongst Quartermaster Sergeants. At times the whole army only had 50 shells in reserve to share amongst the five divisions that made up the Biafran Army. This was when shells were available in reasonable numbers; at other times there were only 10 in store. Requests would come in for 200 shells with no hope of ever receiving more than one or two if they were lucky. When an artillery officer got five shells for his guns he knew that these would only warm up the barrel of one gun. If he wanted to fire a handful of shells he could not hope to get the range of the enemy by using a few rounds to zero in on them. Artillery officers would make up some crisis so that their requests for more shells would go up the list. Even if successful they would be lucky to build up a reserve of 30 shells over a month and these would be used up in an instant. Anti-aircraft crews had the same problem with orders to only use their ammunition when strictly necessary. Nevertheless, they would fire at any aircraft that flew anywhere near their gun positions with no hope of hitting them. When AA gun crews were protecting towns or cities, they were under strong pressure to fire at Nigerian aircraft even if it was only to scare them away. It they fired at the enemy they would get a rapturous round of applause from their admiring public; if they did not fire they could be beaten up or even killed, accused of being saboteurs. The ordinary Biafrans did not understand that firing precious shells at out of range enemy aircraft was a bad idea and this was especially the case when their shells gave away their camouflaged positions to the MiG-17F pilots.

Pistols

Officers in the Biafran Army used a number of automatic pistols and revolvers during the war. Those that had served in the Nigerian army brought their side arms with them with the standard model being the Italian Beretta Model 51. Other older types in service with the pre-1967 Nigerian army were the Browning HP automatic pistol and the Webley MK.IV revolver. The French were reported to have supplied Biafran officers with large numbers of automatic pistols in the summer of 1968. These included the MAS Model 1950 and the MAB P15s, both in 9mm calibre, and older types like the SACM M1935 semi-automatic. Privately, officers admitted that at least one French officer was in Biafra instructing them how to use the weapons, including pistols.[6] In reality many officers, especially the junior ones, were seen armed with rifles, with the vz. 58 assault rifle being the favourite (see below).

Rifles

A weapon often associated with the Biafran Army during the civil war was the Czech-made assault rifle, the vz. 58. The vz. 58 was in frontline service with the Czechoslovakian Army in 1967, having been designed in 1958. While similar in shape to the famous Soviet Kalashnikov, the vz. 58 had a different internal mechanism but retained the distinctive 30-round curved box magazine. This magazine led many observers to confuse the vz. 58 with the iconic Soviet AK-47 which armed most Warsaw Pact countries by the 1960s, as well as many Left-wing guerrilla groups. A reasonable number of these rifles which were imported from Czechoslovakia in early 1967 and they were seen in use with the Biafrans for the whole of the conflict. Another Czech weapon in Biafran service was the older vz. 52 self-loading rifle, which was a poorly designed and manufactured weapon. It had been designed and produced in the

This Red Devil lies on the jungle road with its tracks blown off by Nigerian shell fire and a skull gruesomely stuck on its roof. The machineguns which armed this adapted Bren Gun Carrier would fire through the gap between the original vehicle and the added superstructure. (Leif Hellstron via Al Venter)

Happy Biafran troops stand on top of a Nigerian Army armoured vehicle which has been destroyed in a fire fight. The vehicle is one of the many types produced in workshops by the Biafrans and then captured by the Federals. This was a rare case of Biafran armour being impressed into Nigerian service instead of the other way round. (Albert Grandolini Collection)

short interlude between the end of the world war and the Soviet takeover of Czechoslovakia. It used the Czech 7.62mm M52 round which was not interchangeable with the Soviet M43 round of the same calibre. Unfortunately for the Biafrans the 7.62mm round used in the vz. 58 was not interchangeable with the same calibre round for the vz. 52 either. One round was, frustratingly, shorter than the other and caused more problems for the Biafran logistics officers. Substantial numbers of the vz. 52, with its 10-round box magazine, were seen in use with the Biafrans during the early period of the war but were withdrawn from frontline service after 1967. It was still seen in use, however, as a training weapon as late as July 1968, but by this time all suitable ammunition had probably been expended. At least 1,000 Belgian FN/FAL self-loading rifles were also in service with the Biafrans and were purchased from the British firm Parker Hale at the start of the war. According to their records between 1 – 2,000 FN/FALs were allowed to be exported to Biafra before the arms embargo was enforced. To these must be added a number of FALs captured from the Nigerians, especially during the early part of the war. Also captured in fairly large numbers was the West German made H&K G3 assault rifle which was the standard rifle of the Nigerian Army throughout the war. From photographic evidence it appears that quite a few were in service; and as far as is known, they were highly prized too. G3s were usually issued to NCOs and above, and to the shock platoons of every battalion.

A number of Spanish CETME Model 58 assault rifles, which the H&K G3 was based on, probably also found their way into Biafran service. Outwardly the two look almost identical and rifles which look like the G3 may well have been the Model 58. No exact figures are available on the number of FN/FAL and G3 rifles that were captured by the Biafran Army, but sources like Forsyth state that they made up to 40% of the Biafran weaponry.

The vast majority of Biafran soldiers were, however, armed with one of two Second World War types of vintage bolt action rifles: the German-made Mauser Model 98k and the British Lee-Enfield .303 in either its MKIII or No. 4 versions. Mausers in service with the Biafrans may have been the original German version or one of its many foreign copies, such as the Czech vz. 24 or Belgian FN30. All of the Mausers took 7.92mm bullets which made the procurement of suitable ammunition from abroad a little easier. Lee Enfield No. 4 rifles had been the standard rifle in Nigerian Army service until the mid-1960s. Most of them had been withdrawn however from the east before Biafra's secession and only about 200 of them were

This Federal Saladin armoured car has fallen into an 'elephant trap' type of tank trap which has been carefully prepared on a dirt road. The armoured car has fallen head first into the hole which would have been covered with tarpaulins which had been covered in dirt. Without heavy lifting gear this potential prize for the Biafran Army could not be put back into service. (Author's Collection)

Excited Biafran troops gather around a recently disabled Federal Ferret scout car which appears to have had its wheels blown off by rebel mines. Unfortunately for the Biafrans putting armoured vehicles like this back into action was not always possible and many had to be simply cannibalised for spare parts. This Ferret has already had its main armament machinegun removed from the turret and put back into use by the rebels. (Via Michael Draper)

available at the start of the war. Additional supplies of them were procured either by capture or in the arms shipments that arrived after the start of the war. Although both the Mauser and Lee Enfield were out of date by 1967, the Biafrans were glad of any weaponry and they used both throughout the war. Amongst the rifles captured at the end of the war by the Nigerians were a number of French MAS-36 rifles, which were the standard model in service with the French in 1940. These rifles were in service with a number of former French colonies in Africa in the 1960s and probably came from Gabon or Ivory Coast. Both these countries were alleged to have emptied out of date weapons from their arsenals at the request of the French and given them to the desperate Biafrans. These older weapons were then in all probability replaced by more up to date small arms by the French who could then claim with justification that they had not supplied them directly to Biafra. A number of Soviet Kalashnikov AK-47 assault rifles were also reported in use with the Biafrans and these had been captured from Nigeria. The AK-47 was issued to some Nigerian troops in the latter stages of the war to supplement their standard H&Ks and FN/FALs. During the Biafran siege of Owerri in 1969, the Nigerians air dropped a large number of AK-47s to their besieged troops and many of them fell into rebel hands; after Owerri fell it was noticed that a lot of Biafran officers had suddenly acquired a 'prized' AK-47. The use of the Soviet assault rifle by the Biafrans may have started the rumour that Israel was selling them small arms. It was reported that the Israelis had sold a number of so-called 'obsolete' small arms to the rebels. These were said to be rifles that they had captured during the 1967 Six Day War and may have included Egyptian or Syrian AK-47s. One would assume however that the larger number of older types of Soviet supplied weaponry like the SKS semi-automatic rifle would have been on the list. One source does say that the Israelis pointed the Biafrans in the 'right direction' of the arms dealers who were selling surplus Six Day war booty.

Sub-Machineguns

As with rifles, the Biafrans used an exotic variety of sub-machineguns during the war and these included several obscure Italian models from the late 1940s and early 1950s. The Sten MKI Second World War-vintage sub-machinegun was used by both the Biafran and Nigerian armies. Other models included the US Thompson

The crew of a Biafran Saladin armoured car pose proudly on top of their vehicle in March 1969. Those few former Nigerian armoured vehicles that could be put back into action were like secret weapons in Biafran hands. When Federal troops were faced by their own armoured cars in action the shock factor was often enough to make them run away. On the other side the use of these rare captors by the Biafrans raised morale and were responsible for several major victories by the rebels. (Author's Collection)

seen in service with the 4th Commando Brigade in large numbers. These arrived with the French-supplied weaponry in 1968 and may have come directly from surplus stocks. Surplus British Lanchester M1938 sub-machineguns were similar in design to the German MP-28 and previously had been carried in most British warships' armouries. It was adopted by the Royal Navy for its landing parties and had been seen in use during the Korean War of the early 1950s. The Lanchester was used particularly by the mercenary force which launched the ill-fated attack on the port of Calabar. This type of sub-machinegun would have been in wider service if the aircraft delivering them in 1966 had not crashed en route with nearly 1,000 examples on board (see below). By far the most common types in service with the Biafran army however were the Czechoslovakian vz. 23 and 25s. These modern sub-machineguns were received as part of the main arms shipments in 1967. Some may have been supplied from captured Arab stocks taken during the Six Day War by Israel and then sold on to Biafra. Another rarer Czechoslovakian weapon seen in Biafran hands was the CZ 247, a direct descendent of the CZ1938 model. This sub-machinegun had a 40-round box magazine and was only manufactured in small numbers. Its unusual feature was that although the magazine was normally vertical under the gun it could be turned to the side in a 'sten-like' fashion.

Machineguns

The majority of imported machineguns in Biafran service came from Czechoslovakian sources, with the Type 53 the main heavy type in service. This Second World War gun originated in 1937 and was intended to be the standard medium machinegun of the Czechoslovakian Army. After the takeover of Czechoslovakia in 1938 most were taken over by the German Army while others were used by the Slovakian Army which was allied to the Germans. Two types of modern Czech light machineguns were also included in the early arms deals done with Czechoslovakia. These were the vz. 52 light machinegun and the vz. 59 general purpose machinegun, both of which used the old 7.62mm round. Although the number of these up-to-date machineguns in service cannot have been too large they were seen in widespread use. Another older Czech type in service was the venerable Zb 30 light machinegun; this was the ground-breaking weapon developed by the British into the better known Bren Gun. Probably also from Czech sources came a number of the famous German MG34 machinegun. These were probably taken into Czech service as 'war booty' at the end of the Second World War and were included in the arms shipments from Prague. Towards the end of the war large shipments of weaponry of French origin came into Biafra from Gabon and the Ivory Coast. Amongst these shipments were a number of elderly Chatelleraut M1924/29 light machineguns which were the standard light machinegun of the French Army in the Second World War. Captured machineguns in Biafran service were mainly of two types, the West German MG42/59 light machinegun and the Belgian made FN GPMG. The former was basically the famous MG42 of German Second World War fame modified to fire the 7.62mm NATO round. At the start of the civil war the MG42/59 was the standard light machinegun of the Nigerian Federal Army but was supplemented by the L7A2 as the war progressed. FN GPMGs and the British L7A2 GPMG were the standard General-Purpose Machineguns in a number of NATO countries. During the course of the war the GPMGs superseded the MG42/59 and machineguns captured towards the end of the war would probably be of the former type. A handful of Bren .303 light machineguns were on the strength of the Biafran Army at the start of the war and these would have been supplemented by both captured Nigerian and imported examples. Any captured machineguns were usually reliant for ammunition on Nigerian sources as the arms embargo imposed by the Western powers on Biafra made it difficult to import ammunition from other sources.

Anti-Tank Rocket Launchers

The 15 modern, Swedish-made Carl Gustav anti-tank weapons bought by Nigeria in the early 1960s had all been evacuated away from the east already in 1966. Thus, the Biafrans started the war with next to no conventional anti-tank weapons and relied on hand-held rocket launchers instead.

The Biafrans acquired a number of Czechoslovakian made P-27 'Pancervoka' rocket launchers, which were based on the Soviet RPG-2 – a predecessor to the more famous RPG-7. They also reportedly had Chinese Type-56 versions of the RPG-2 but there is no photographic evidence of this. According to one US eyewitness,

Biafran troops move towards the frontline carrying their locally made 'Ojukwu Kettles' on their heads. These primitive but usually highly affective weapons would be placed against the base of a tree or wall at the side of a road. They would be then camouflaged to hide them from the advancing Nigerians who usually moved down jungle roads. When set off the kettles which were filled with smashed glass, nut and bolts and other scrap metal would spray the oncoming Federal troops with their deadly contents. Against troops on foot or in trucks or Land Rovers the results could be devastating causing death and serious injuries. (Author's Collection)

the Biafrans had a fatal habit of firing the Chinese Type 56 from the wrong shoulder. Biafran soldiers fired the rocket launcher from the left shoulder and a gas ejection port was on the right of the tube; when the rocket was fired a flame shot out of the exhaust port with fatal consequences for the unfortunate soldier.[7]

The Biafrans had little or no instruction of the use of their rocket launchers in 1968 but eventually learned how to operate them. Of course, because of the haphazard way that arms arrived – without instruction manuals and usually without any instructors – such incidents were bound to happen.

Another Czechoslovakian anti-tank weapon which appears to have been used in small numbers was the T-21 82mm recoilless gun. This weapon fired a fin-stabilised HEAT projectile and was capable of penetrating up to 230mm of armour, which would have made it deadly against anything in Nigerian service. One example is on display at the Nigerian War Museum.

The Biafrans also had a number of 37mm SNEB rocket launchers which they reportedly received from Portuguese sources. During 1969 they were also supplied with a number of French anti-tank weapons, which were reported to be SARPAC launchers. This more sophisticated weapon was harder to use and so two instructors were reported to have gone to Biafra to give their operators a crash course.

The Soviet RPG-7 was in service with the Federal Army and a few were also seen in the hands of Biafran troops but not in any great numbers. Also acquired by the Biafrans were Second World War-era rifle grenades which were bought in some numbers. Unfortunately, when they arrived, they did not have the adapters which were needed to make them operable from the muzzles of Biafran Lee Enfield rifles.

Biafran Artillery

In the early days of the war Ojukwu had promised his officers artillery and other heavy weaponry, which was supposed to be arriving on the 'next shipment' but often didn't materialise. Even when artillery pieces were listed on the manifest of an arms shipment they rarely appeared. As with other armaments, the Biafrans' desperation for artillery was exploited by the arms dealers who knew that their clients had to trust their word – which was often broken.

In the kind of jungle fighting that took place during this war the obvious light artillery weapon for the Biafrans to use was the infantry mortar. As with every other type of weaponry there were never enough mortars to go around and even when they were available ammunition for them was scarce. The first two models used by the Biafrans were the British Army's 2-inch and 3-inch weapons which had been taken from Nigerian Army stores. The larger calibre British 4.2-inch Chemical Mortar was also reported to be in service but this may have been a single example. Other types of mortars seen in service were the Spanish made 81mm L-N and the French 120mm. Both types were always short of ammunition with one journalist saying that the 120mm weapons only had 2 shells available each during a battle.[8] If there was a particularly serious crisis at the front some mortars could be taken from the central stores and rushed to a threatened sector. For instance, when a unit of mercenaries under the command of Captain Le Rois fought an important defensive battle on the Onitsha front in 1968, Ojukwu sent six precious 81mm mortars to the sector with 300 bombs: an unprecedented amount in the war.

The exact number of artillery pieces in use with the Biafrans is difficult to estimate as different sources mention various types in service. Certainly, some Italian made 105mm pack howitzers were captured by the Biafrans from the Nigerians and put into service against their former masters. For instance, during the fighting for the Biafran capital of Enugu in early October 1967, it was claimed that several 105mm artillery pieces were captured. The British 6-pounder anti-tank gun (introduced into service in 1942) was on the strength of the small pre-war Nigerian artillery arm. Several captured 6-pounder guns were used by the Biafrans and these included one left behind by the Nigerians when they retreated from the town of Oguta. Another 6-pounder was photographed in an August 1968 news report in which it is described simply as a 'captured Biafran cannon.'[9] Another example of this anti-tank gun was seen in action during the 'liberation' of Owerri in 1969. Rolf Steiner claimed that his unit had four 105mm howitzers in its arsenal, and four 'Krupp' 105mm field guns. The latter might have been of Czechoslovak origin, as one artillery piece captured from the Biafrans appears to have been an M18/49: a Czechoslovakian upgrade of the German-made 105mm LeFH 18/40, with solid rubber tyres. A few of these may well have been imported in the early days of the war along with the shipments of other Czechoslovak arms.

The Biafrans, according to Frederick Forsyth, also imported a few First World War vintage field guns which were totally unusable.[10] Some of the precious field guns that the Biafrans did manage to import often arrived without sights and other parts. According to another source a few pieces of Swiss-made artillery that were bought by the Biafrans were found to be completely rusted up on arrival and were useless. Reports from 1968 also claimed that the Biafrans had acquired 'heavy artillery' but this was just another example of false rumours that were prevalent during the war.

Shells were always in short supply and major offensives were frequently launched with a stockpile of only two rounds for each of the available guns – and even this only after the Biafrans had carefully collected shells for a few weeks before. Even when this pre-offensive rationing took place the paltry amount of shells that the Biafrans had managed to save were soon exhausted.

A typical rocket crew moves forward with the lead man carrying the launching tube on his head in West African style in 1968. Behind him are his three comrades each carrying a heavy metal rocket with large fins at the back and smaller stabilising fins just underneath the warhead. Underneath the launching tube can be seen the metal frame which formed a basic stand to fire the rockets from. When there was a shortage of small arms unarmed men could be allocated to rocket units to act as porters until rifles became available. (Author's Collection)

Anti-Aircraft Guns

The Biafrans were woefully short of anti-aircraft guns and had to rely almost entirely on captured weaponry. Several ex-Nigerian Bofors 40mm AA guns were used by the Biafrans with one being captured at the fall of the lakeside town of Oguta, along with a good supply of shells. The retreating Nigerians had pushed the gun and other equipment into the lake, leaving them behind for the grateful Biafrans to recover. Rolf Steiner in his autobiography says that the Italian mercenary Norbiatto captured and dismounted two Oerlikon 20mm anti-aircraft guns from Nigerian freighters and these presumably were put into service with the Biafran Army.[11]

A 20mm Oerlikon was also captured at Bori and would have been used until the stock of shells ran out. During an operation behind Nigerian lines in 1968 a further two light anti-aircraft guns along with ammunition were captured and brought back to

A rocket crew which is part of a Biafran 'Strike Force' prepares to go out on an operation. There must have been a well organised production line for the rockets which appear to have been made to a specification. From photographic evidence it appears that rockets were readily available when all other heavy weaponry was in short supply. (Author's Collection)

Curious Biafran troops gather around one of their home-made rocket launchers as one of the crew prepares to put the rocket into the primitive launching tube. Although the shrapnel filled rockets could cause casualties when on target they were difficult to aim with any accuracy. With no aiming mechanism the rocket was simply pointed in the direction of the enemy and the fuse was lit. Like a giant deadly firework, the rocket could sometimes go off course and head back towards the soldiers who had fired it! Often just the unexpected noise of the rocket going off was enough to terrify the Federal troops who assumed that the Biafrans did not have artillery. (Author's Collection)

Biafran Army, Military Police and Naval personnel stand guard over boxes and metal containers full of precious ammunition flown in to the country in 1968. On the right of the photograph are canisters containing British 76mm shells for any captured Nigerian Saladin armoured cars. To the left are boxes of Spanish 7.62 mm ammunition which will be used in the various types of rifles in service with the Biafran Army. (Mike Draper)

A soldier holds up a box of 7.62mm ammunition for the camera as his unit prepares to go out on an operation. To his left a comrade holds up an RPG-7 anti-tank rocket launcher which may have been captured from the Federal Army. Most units would have been lucky to have one anti-tank weapon and the RPG-7 and its various foreign copies were highly prized by the Biafrans. Before launching an offensive the Biafran Army's logistical officers would squirrel away as much ammunition as possible. (Albert Grandolini Collection)

be used by the Biafran Army. As with all captured weaponry, the Biafrans would have had difficulty acquiring the correct ammunition and spare parts for these guns from the arms market. A few light anti-aircraft guns were, according to some sources, flown in on the night-time supply flights and these most likely came from Swiss sources. According to reports a few 'factory rejected' Hispana-Suiza 20mm anti-aircraft guns which should have been melted down were sold to Biafra. They were officially part of an order to the USA but somehow found their way to France and were then included in arms shipments to Biafra.[12] Even though there was a shortage of ammunition for all their guns the Biafran anti-aircraft artillery, like their Nigerian counterparts, had a habit of firing at any plane that flew over their positions. This included larger aircraft that were flying well out of range of the light guns the Biafrans had. The best anti-aircraft guns and crew were reserved for Ojukwu's villa complex in the town of Umuahia, which acted as the Biafran seat of government for most of the war. Ojukwu's residence was targeted several times by Nigerian Air Force MiG-17-Fs during the war and for that reason it was relatively well protected by light anti-aircraft guns. The majority of anti-aircraft guns were concentrated as the war wore on at the vital Uli airfield where three Bofors 40mm, four Oerlikon 20mm and a large number of machineguns were based.

Biafran Armoured Vehicles

Before the war began the Biafrans were well aware that in any coming conflict they would be faced by the Federal Army's armoured might. Ferret scout cars armed with Browning machineguns and Saladin heavy armoured cars with 76mm guns were already in service.

The Biafrans captured several French-supplied Panhard armoured cars from the Nigerians. The example shown here on the left is an AML-60 armed with a 60mm mortar. Named 'Oguta Boy' after the lakeside town where it was captured the Panhard was a welcome addition to their armoured force. A number of Nigerian Daimler Ferret scout cars, as shown on the right, armed with Browning machineguns were captured by the Biafrans and some were put back into action by them. Most only saw short service before being destroyed or put out of action by the enemy, with only one, 'Uzuakoli Boy' seeing long service. (Artworks by David Bocquelet)

This ex-Nigerian Saladin armoured car with its 76mm main armament, named 'Corporal Nwafor' after the man who died capturing it, operated on several fronts during the war. Sometimes its mere appearance at the front was enough to terrify the Nigerians who did not expect to face this kind of weapon. (Artwork by David Bocquelet)

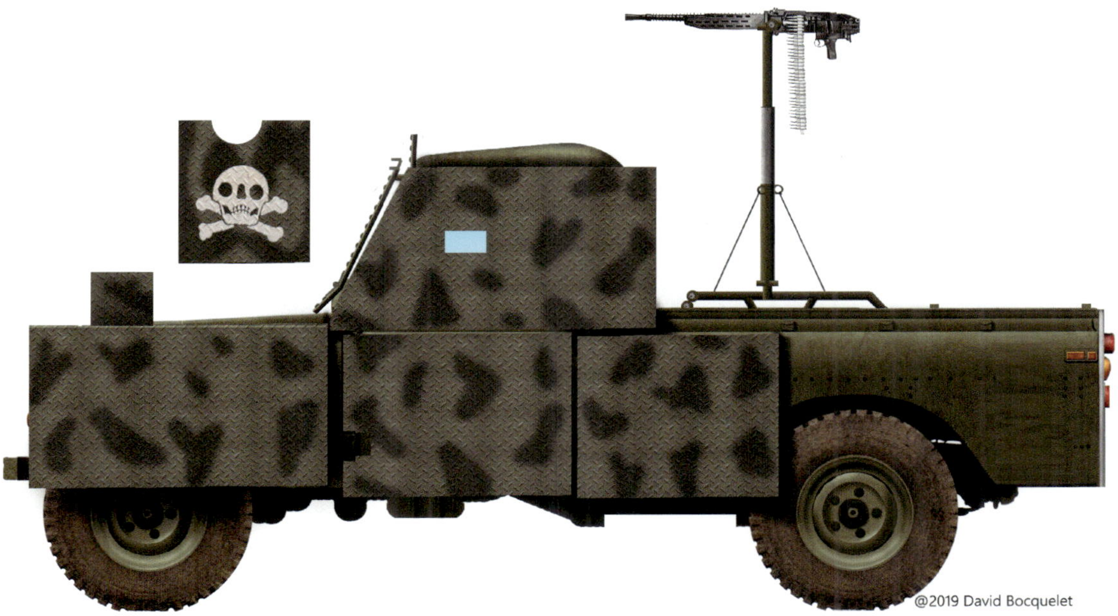

The 4th Commando Brigade had at least one of these Land Rovers converted by local workshops to create an improvised armoured car. This example was armed with a Czech ZB-53 heavy machinegun and had the skull and crossbones unit symbol stencilled on the front. Nowhere in the history of the 4th Brigade is it mentioned that the unit had its own armoured element but this vehicle was seen in several press photographs. (Artwork by David Bocquelet)

There were at least a dozen Universal Carriers bought by the Biafrans and converted into light tanks by local workshops. This model – locally dubbed the Red Devil – had no turret but had an open front with mountings for at least one light machinegun fitted. In reality these Red Devils were 'death traps' for their crews and most were quickly disabled by Nigerian artillery. (Artwork by David Bocquelet)

This model of improvised armoured car was built around a Land Rover or station wagon chassis and made use of sloped armour to try and make it more bullet resistant. It is not known if the turret was fixed but, with the limited tools and equipment available, it was probably armed with a single forward facing machinegun as its main armament. At least two of this model of armoured car were made and were used in operations alongside Red Devils. (Artwork by David Bocquelet)

It was reported that the Biafrans converted more than one bulldozer into an armoured vehicle. This example was captured by the Nigerians after being disabled by their artillery during fighting in June 1968. Because of its added superstructure the top speed of the 'tank' was a mere 2 miles an hour instead of its usual 5. (Artwork by David Bocquelet)

The least-well-known Biafran aircraft were two North American B-25J Mitchell light bombers (44-31491 and 44-29919), which arrived in the territory in October 1967: both were effectively lost during the same mission – an air strike on Calabar airfield, on 2 December. Their armament – including four or five machineguns fitted into the nose – was slightly more potent than that of the B-26s. Both received a camouflage pattern, probably in olive green or dark blue, with grey-green or olive green softly outlined in black on upper surfaces and sides. Undersurfaces were painted either in light grey or light blue. (Artwork by Tom Cooper)

The first of the Biafran Invader light bombers was a this former US Air Force and French Air Force B-26R, serial number 41-39531. It was painted in olive green overall on which a disruptive camouflage pattern in grey-green was crudely sprayed (a further developed variant of this pattern eventually became something like 'standard' for early aircraft of the Biafran Air Force) and flown by the famous Polish adventurer Jean Zumbach. The aircraft received the fierce sharkmouth insignia but was actually armed only with a single machinegun installed in its former radome, and light bombs. Last flown on 21 August 1967 (probably on an air raid on Kano Air Base), it was subsequently captured almost intact by federal troops at Enugu airport. (Artwork by Tom Cooper)

The second Biafran Invader was this former French Air Force RB-26P (originally registered as F-BMJR in France) with a perspex nose. As far as is known, it was outfitted with 24 underwing launch rails for unguided rockets only. Available photographs show it as probably painted in dark blue, with a camouflage pattern in olive green with a very soft, black outline on upper surfaces and sides, and light grey on undersurfaces. This Invader suffered from frequent engine snags and it remains unknown if it ever received the full Biafran Air Force insignia on the fin. (Artwork by Tom Cooper)

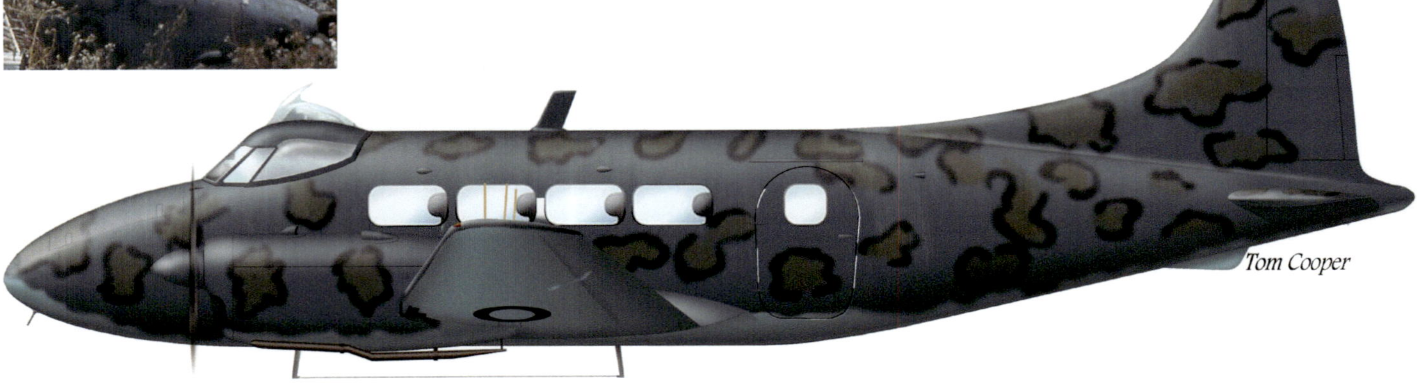

This DH.104 Riley Dove (construction number 04246, formerly registered as 5N-AGF) was requisitioned by the Biafrans from the Bristow Helicopter Company on 18 July 1967 and then used to transport Biafran personnel around the territory. It was camouflaged in dark blue, with a camouflage pattern in olive green with a very soft, black outline on top surfaces and sides, and light blue on undersurfaces (reportedly, the same colours in which the sole Biafran Fokker F.27 was camouflaged). The aircraft ground-looped at Uli airfield, hit a truck damaging a propeller and was declared a write-off. Eventually, it was deposited on a nearby school playground, where it was often photographed. (Artwork by Tom Cooper)

The Biafrans acquired a total of 12 T-6Gs from French sources in late 1967, but these took much too long to be shipped to Lisbon, then overhauled, and flown into the territory: indeed, only four are known to have been delivered at all. This example – USAF serial 51-14810 – was abandoned in Biafra in January 1970, captured by the Federals, flown out to Lagos, and then scrapped sometimes after May 1972. Its camouflage colours consisted of black overall, atop of which a disruptive pattern in dark brown and olive green was applied – on top surfaces and sides only – and it wore no national markings or other insignia at all. (Artwork by Tom Cooper)

All the Biafran MFI-9B Minicons were painted in gloss green and black on top surfaces and sides, and light grey on undersurfaces, applied crudely with help of brush, in a pattern that differed from aircraft to aircraft. The first batch wore serials BB101 to BB105. The second batch should have been serialled as BB903, BB905, BB907 and BB099, but this remains unconfirmed. Their tie-ups with Swedish identities remain unknown. The example shown to the left received a small Biafran flag on the fuselage side, too: BB105 was eventually captured and brought to Lagos. The example to the right is shown wearing a roundel in Biafran national markings on the rear fuselage: it remains unknown exactly how many of the MFI-9Bs received such markings. All aircraft were armed with two French-made pods for 68mm unguided rockets: the installation of these required no extra work because this variant was designed with built-in hardpoints. (Artwork by Tom Cooper)

Biafran Militiaman, Enugu, 1967
In order to support the army, Biafra's government created a militia based in the main towns and cities of the country, formed from men and women with little training and almost no weaponry. This young volunteer proudly wears a t-shirt with a flashy patriotic slogan and makeshift military style trousers. The only military item he wears is a light khaki field cap, locally known as the 'Fidel cap', with a metal badge pinned to the front. Note his Chinese-made red sneakers and how his trousers have been tucked into his socks in imitation of military gaiters. His old double-barrelled shotgun seemed unfit for combat, but it was really the best that the militia had. (Artwork by Anderson Subtil)

Colonel Joseph 'Hannibal' Achuzia, Commander 'S' Division, Owerri, March 1969.
The illustration depicts Col. Achuzia while in charge of the elite 'S' Division. He is shown here wearing a locally made 'Duck Hunter' camouflage tunic with the rank insignia of Colonel and collar tabs in the British style. High on his sleeves he displays the iconic Biafran rising-sun patch and the 'S' Division's lightning flash patch (see inset). Another influence leftover from the British presence in the pre-1960 Nigerian Army was the use of swagger sticks, favoured by officers on both sides. The Service Cap is much the same as the one used by Nigerian officers, but it has the embroidered Biafran Army badge (see inset) affixed to the front. (Artwork by Anderson Subtil)

Major Rolf Steiner, 4th Commando Brigade, 1968
As a veteran of the former 1er régiment étranger de parachutistes, Steiner is shown here with the parachutist beret of the Foreign Legion and displays his French jump wings on his right chest. His jacket appears to be of a locally produced model using French or Portuguese 'Lizard' camouflage pattern, but the trousers are certainly of the M1947 uniform worn by French troops in Indochina. The 4th Commando Brigade 'skull-and-crossbones' patch is worn beneath the rising-sun patch on both sleeves, and Major rank badges on the shoulder straps. The holster of his 9mm Browning Hi-Power semi-automatic pistol and M56 canvas belt are of French Army origin. (Artwork by Anderson Subtil)

Biafran Soldier, 12th Division, 1969
This illustration shows the extent of improvisation within the Biafran Army: this soldier is shown wearing a khaki shirt from the uniform initially distributed to the Biafran troops, and trousers of some later fabricated uniform, where a makeshift camouflage pattern has been painted on. Like most of his companions he has bare feet, but his head is protected by a US M1 steel helmet taken from a Nigerian corpse or prisoner. On his belt, probably acquired the same way, he has two magazine bags, one of British origin and one from Czechoslovakia as is his vz. 58 rifle. (artwork by Anderson Subtil)

A photograph of Colonel Ojukwu showing him wearing the peaked officer's cap which was distinct in having a red feather hackle at the front. The image of immaculately dressed Biafran officers commanding soldiers wearing rags was not lost on the world's press. In reality some ordinary Biafran troops were well uniformed while other officer's uniforms were worn out and patched. Ojukwu ordered that any officer with spare uniform items must give them to other officers who did not have a full uniform. (Author's Collection

Alexander Gay, a Scottish veteran of the Congo, took part in the mercenary revolt at Bakavu in 1967. When he got to Biafra he became a friend of Colonel Steiner and then went on to serve as Taffy Williams' second in command in late 1968. Gay wears his beret from his service with the Congolese Army in the mid-1960s and has the green scarf of the 4th Commando Brigade/Division. (Author's Collection)

Armand 'The Brave' Ianarelli the Corsican mercenary who, like most of his comrades, had served in the French Foreign Legion in the 1950s and early 1960s is seen here in 1969. He was known as one of the bravest of the mercenaries and was admired by his fellow officers. Ianarelli was also a humanitarian who secretly gave his salary to local missionaries to help feed starving children. (Private Collection)

Biafran Army trainees undergo a bit of 'square bashing' in the early stages of their short training course. These recruits are being trained at a camp near to the Biafran wartime capital Umuahia in 1968. It was frustrating for many recruits that they had to make do with staves or sticks when training. They would often have to go off to the front without a rifle and then would hopefully be issued with one taken from a wounded or killed soldier. (Author's Collection)

This Biafran soldier belongs to a battalion-sized unit taking part in a raid behind Nigerian lines in 1969. The weapons carried by this unit included FN FALs and H&K G-3s but the majority are armed with bolt action Mausers. In most cases the FALs and G-3s were captured from the Nigerians and tended to be carried by experienced privates, NCOs and junior officers. His uniform is a light khaki cotton type with the typical field cap which was produced in large numbers in local workshops. (Authors Collection)

Young commandos of the 4th Commando Brigade are seen during jungle training in the summer of 1968. Although the two soldiers who are both armed with Mauser 7.62mm rifles wear the duck hunter type camouflage uniforms, neither appears to have been issued with the unit's distinctive skull and crossbones arm patch. One man had drawn crude versions of the skull and crossbones on the peak of his cap with a marker pen. (Private Collection)

The Biafran Army putting a selection of captured Federal army weapons and ammunition on display as a propaganda exercise. Star of the display was this 105mm pack howitzer which, according to the plaque on its side, was captured in the battle for Port Harcourt. Although a few cases of 105mm shells were captured with this gun, once they were used up the Biafrans depended on capturing more from the Nigerians. (Author's Collection)

A launcher for the Ogbinigwe exploding mine called the 'Marshal' is seen as a post-war exhibit at the Nigerian War Museum. Like a cross between a primitive mortar and an oversized shotgun the Marshal could be a devastating weapon. It was intended that its explosive charge would be shot into the air over the advancing enemy and when it exploded the shrapnel would rain down on the enemy. (via author)

The damaged B-26R is examined at Enugu airport after its front tyre burst when it landed from a mission in the summer of 1967. It was towed off the runway so that other aircraft of the tiny Biafran air force could land. At this point in the war there was little danger of attacks from the still organising Nigerian Air Force. The burst tyre kept this aircraft out of the war for a week until another one could be found to replace it. Biafra's early bombers were given mystical status by the public who saw them as the saviours of the secessionist state in the early war period. (via author)

Two ground crew personnel attaching French Matra rocket launchers to the wing of an MFI-9 at their forward base in Gabon. The MFI-9B still has its civilian paint work and hasn't received camouflage colours yet. After having hardpoints for rocket launchers fitted in Paris they were dismantled and then flown into the pro-Biafran West African state of Gabon. They were then assembled and prepared for their next move to a bush airstrip in Biafra where they could begin operations. (Via Albert Grandolini)

As the MFI-9B pilots prepare to go on their first mission in late May 1969, they all got together to camouflage their aircraft with Volkswagen car paints. To the left, Count von Rosen can be seen stripped to his waist with paint brush in hand. Air raids by these tiny aircraft proved major morale boosters for the Biafran Army, who had suffered from hundreds of NAF air strikes during the war. (Author's Collection)

A newly painted MFI-9B prepares to take off on an early mission over Nigerian lines in the summer of 1969. This particular aircraft has not had its rocket launchers fitted yet. Five aircraft were delivered but no more than four ever flew on a single mission. One aircraft may have been left unarmed to act as a spotter. (Pierre Mens Via Mike Draper)

The south-eastern part of Nigeria, with the area claimed by the secessionists as Biafra (shaded zone), in May 1967. (Map by Tom Cooper)

Young soldiers examine a recently captured mortar bomb as if it is a rare and precious thing. Their comrades look over their shoulder to get a look at the bomb which may or may not fit any mortars their unit has. Whenever possible any unsuitable weapons or ammunition would be moved to a headquarters where it would be kept until suitable weapons could be located. The soldiers are well uniformed for 1969 and may be wearing captured Nigerian Army uniforms like the M2 steel helmet the man on the right has on. (Albert Grandolini Collection)

Of course, none of the pre-war armoured vehicles were in the east when the fighting started. Determined to 'meet might with might' the Biafrans looked at how they could counter what was to prove to be a decisive advantage for the Nigerians. They had no anti-tank capability as their handful of British 6-pounder guns were being used as conventional artillery pieces.

Improvised Armoured Vehicles

Desperate attempts to buy modern armoured vehicles to counter the Nigerian Ferrets and Saladins came to nothing even if the Biafran agents continued to scour surplus dealers and even junkyards all over Europe, and thus the Biafrans decided to improvise their own. The information on resulting vehicles is sketchy, but it is known that several Land Rovers and trucks were fitted with steel plates. For example, a Port Harcourt automotive assembly plant made several 'tanks' which were civilian trucks with metal plates added. A metal plate box type structure was fitted to the rear of the 15cwt trucks and their cabs were also covered with a metal skin. Firing ports with opening shutters were added to the main body and also in the front and side of the cab. The extra weight added to the existing weight of the truck put a strain on the trucks' engines which led to them overheating after a short period. One of these vehicles was seen after its destruction during the fighting at Ikem and Obollo Eke in 1967: it looked similar to something produced during the Spanish Civil War some 30 years before.

Other improvised armoured vehicles were produced, with one going by the name 'Genocide,' having a top speed of just 10 miles-per-hour due to its excessive weight. Another one was faster: when seen for the only recorded time it was outfitted with side-skirts that almost touched the ground and it could reach a speed of up to 40 miles-per-hour.

Armament of such improvised vehicles varied: Land Rovers deployed for the Mid-West offensive in the summer of 1967 carried a machinegun on their rear deck, as did two 20-ton armoured cars which spearheaded the 'armoured' column involved. Another home-made 'armoured Land Rover' had a cylindrical turret – that was probably not rotatable – with a machinegun fitted to it, and seems to have been produced in some numbers as two were photographed while operated by the Red Devils (see below for details).

The 4th Commando Brigade had at least one armoured Land Rover in 1968 which was used as a staff vehicle. The Biafrans also added armoured superstructures to several bulldozers, which were each armed with at least one machinegun.

The Red Devils

During the early months of the war the Biafrans had managed to acquire via several sources a number of old Vickers Bren or Universal Carriers.[13] These lightly armoured, open topped tracked vehicles had been used by the Allies during the war to move infantry or tow artillery around the battlefield and had been armed with a single Bren light machinegun at the front. They were only expected to provide a limited amount of protection for their passengers and were certainly not expected of take on other armoured vehicles. Dubbed 'Red Devils' by the Biafrans, the Bren Gun Carriers were fitted locally with a clumsy looking armoured superstructure which nearly doubled their height – and weight. The converted 'Red Devils' came in two main models: one without a turret and one with a circular turret armed with a light machinegun. Models without turrets had an open front to allow a machinegun to fire from it, while the turreted version had a machinegun fixed forward. Both models had two hatches on each side to fire small arms from, and a door at the rear for getting into the vehicle. Massively overweight, Red Devils regularly overheated in action and had to be 'rested' every 30 minutes – to allow the engine and the transmission to cool down. This not only severely limited their operational capabilities, but also limited their nominal 30-miles-per-hour speed to a crawl.

Red Devils were used in a number of engagements with the Nigerians in the early months of the war and most were knocked out in combat. Although the armoured plating gave some protection against small arms fire it was virtually useless against Federal recoilless rifles and other artillery pieces: unsurprisingly, despite the proud boasts, they usually turned out to be death traps for their crews.

The Biafrans were reported to have lost all their improvised armoured vehicles and their Red Devils in the early fighting: only four are known to have taken part in the Mid-West invasion around September 1967, and few additional ones were deployed in the north. The handful of survivors were shown to a news-crew in 1968, still in working condition, but with a smaller superstructure that gave them a more compact appearance.

The Biafrans did try to buy other armoured cars and scout cars throughout Europe, but with little success – and this although the armies in Europe were in the process of renewing their WWII-era arsenals at the time. Apart from Bren Gun Carriers, they acquired a Daimler Mk.II Dingo scout car from a scrap dealer in Great Britain, but the vehicle broke down on the way to the docks due to the failure of its water pump.[14]

Captured Armoured Vehicles

The Biafrans totally relied on the Federal army as a source of modern armoured vehicles by capturing a number during the war. Many of the captured vehicles were too badly damaged to be put into Biafran service, however, whilst others were caught in elephant traps and could not be recovered due to a lack of lifting gear.

Amongst the first vehicles to be captured and put into Biafran service was a Saladin armoured car. It was taken from the Nigerian 2nd Division and named 'Corporal Nwafor' after the Biafran soldier who died in taking it. 'Corporal Nwafor' was the most effective of such acquisitions and its presence in the field decided several battles. It was eventually put out of action by the Federal army during the battle for Ohoba in July 1969 and its loss was felt throughout Biafra.

Another armoured car which was highly affective was a Panhard AML-60 captured by the Biafrans outside the lakeside town of Oguta in September 1968. It was named 'Oguta Boy' and remained in service until destroyed during the Battle of Uzuakoli in April 1969. An AML-90 was captured too, and seen while guarding Colonel Ojukwu's HQ, but there is no evidence that it ever served on the frontlines – probably due to a lack of spares.

Other types of armoured vehicle employed by the Biafrans were a Saracen armoured personnel carrier captured in Uzuakoli in the same action in which 'Oguta Boy' was lost, and named 'Ndidi' ('patience'). Several Ferret scout cars were captured by the Biafrans during the war but in most cases the vehicles were beyond repair. The only one that was documented as being put into service with them was 'Uzuakoli Boy', which again was captured, as its name suggests, during fighting for Uzuakoli.

Home-Made Weaponry

At the start of the war the Biafrans had gathered together a number of scientists and engineers to produce weapons for the army. Doctor Opkala from Nsukku University was put in charge of the mix of scientists and other experts. He was known during the war as 'Doctor X' to protect his identity from Nigerian authorities. They were formed into the 'Department of Research and Production' – or RAP – and got to work producing a wide variety of homemade weapons. Personnel for RAP came from the University of Nigeria, the Ministry of Communications, the Nigerian Coal Corporation and the Ministry of Works. They were joined by a group of experts and scientists who met regularly at a library in Enugu. This group of scientists looked at developing biological and chemical weapons and some mustard gas was developed. The main products that eventually came off the RAP production lines were homemade means of delivering explosives. Because of the chronic shortage of conventional weaponry in the Biafran Army these locally designed and produced weapons took on a great importance. Biafran technicians became experts in producing weapons often made out of scrap metal and spare parts. One journalist summarised the weaponry produced by RAP during the war, 'RAP's workshops have turned out a variety of devices, among them multiple rocket launchers for anti-aircraft defence, grenades, small arms ammunition, 60mm, 81mm and 120mm mortars with mortar bombs; four varieties of anti-personnel and armoured piercing land mine.'[15] The gunsmiths from the town of Akwa were renowned for producing hunting guns known as 'dane guns' from scratch in the primitive workshops. When the war began they tried to increase production of these 'one shot' guns but it was difficult to access the machinery to do this. What guns they did produce were given to the Militia and Civil Defenders in the summer of 1967. Primitive pistols and revolvers were also made but the quality of the materials they were made from often made them dangerous to fire. There was also confusion over which weapons were imported types and which were homemade. In reality even the so-called munitions experts in the Biafran Army did not know the origin of many of the weapons arriving in small batches by plane during the war.

Ogbunigwes

Foremost amongst the improvised weaponry used by the Biafrans was the 'Ogbunigwe' or 'Mass Killer' – 'Destroyer of All' and its derivatives. The Ogbunigwe was basically a milk churn or bucket shaped cast iron funnel which had explosives placed at its base. The container was then filled with nails and any type of scrap metal and broken glass. Explosive materials used for the charge included liquids – including petrol – enclosed in plastic and sealed to avoid evaporation. These liquid explosive capsules placed in the base of the weapon would then be separated from dry explosives by a thin cardboard layer. Dry explosives were then added on top and finally the weapon was filled to the brim with the scrap metal and glass. At the top of the weapon a thin metal plate was bolted or screwed on to keep the contents inside and to add to the pressure produced when the explosive charge was ignited. In theory the heavy metal casement allowed the explosive pressure to build up before blowing its contents out at great force. To add to the deadly pressure of the Obunigwe, its base was often placed against a tree stump to absorb the recoil and send more explosive power out of the front of the weapon. Others would be positioned at the side of the road or in the ground and then camouflaged with leaves. When a suitable target appeared, the weapon would be fired by means of leads which led from the firer's hidden position. The charge was ignited when a circuit was formed by the leads which were fastened to the negative and positive points of a battery. In turn, these leads were connected to holes drilled in the Ogbunigwe's casement, a charge ran through the explosives and ignited them. Scientists said the weapon worked based on the physics of the 'Monroe Effect' using 'effect percussion and dispersal of shrapnel.'[16]

When used properly, the Ogbunigwes were set up in ambush positions with the weapons let off at intervals to catch the enemy in well-co-ordinated 'killing fields'. Of course, the Nigerians became wary of walking into traps using the weapon and would try and scout ahead to spot them before they could fire. Although most Ogbunigwes were used as ground weapons another version was known as the 'Marshal.' The idea of the Marshal was that one charge would throw the projectile into the air and a second charge would then send shrapnel down upon the enemy. It was adopted into Biafran use towards the end of the war and was seen as a 'secret weapon' by the rebels. A group of visiting British officials on a tour of Biafran lines in December 1969 saw one of the Marshals ready to be used. It was mounted on a primitive looking launching pad and was described as; 'A huge barrel that looked like a medieval siege gun…[it] threw a terrible explosive charge and liquid flame all over the approaching enemy.'[17]

The Marshal had a 7ft long barrel and a 13-inch diameter projectile with a large warhead at the top. It could travel up to 60ft and was timed to detonate at about 50ft above the target.

Ogbunigwes came in various sizes and had a slight variation in design and were manufactured locally in workshops. According to a Biafran official they were producing 500 Obunigwes per day at the height of its production. He also said the weapon had a range of half a mile and had 60 degrees killing zone when used at close quarters. Although its effectiveness may have been exaggerated by some commentators it was widely reported that it could kill or maim up to 60 troops in one blast.

A Biafran soldier carries four H&K G-3 assault rifles which have recently been captured from an ambushed Nigerian patrol. The G-3 became the most common type of rifle used by the Federal Army and was seen in widespread use by the Biafrans. As the war dragged on any attacks on Nigerian units by the Biafrans were usually motivated by the desire to capture arms and equipment. (Albert Grandolini Collection)

Rockets

As well as conventional artillery the Biafrans used a number of crude rockets which could be used against ground or airborne targets. Biafran scientists of the RAP group invented surface-to-surface rockets that were fired in the general direction of the enemy. The first testing of 3ft long rockets did not go well with six exploding when they were launched, causing some casualties. A 6-inch version was more successful but only flew for 200 yards during testing and the rusty mild steel they were made from was inadequate. When the teething problems were sorted out the new 18-inch version eventually had a range of 2 miles although some claimed it could fly for 10 miles. These new workshops made rockets about 18-inches long and 3-inches diameter were made by cannibalising explosives from dud Nigerian shells and rockets fired at the Biafrans. Ground to air missiles were also made by the Biafrans and had the same 'hit or miss' performance. The rockets were fired either from a tripod stand made from metal tubing or in a more transportable form from a hollow tube. In the tripod method of firing the rocket, two pieces of metal tubing formed a track on which the projectile was placed at a slightly raised angle. When the crew withdrew from the firing stand they ignited the charge at the base of the rocket and stood back. It was then fired from the stand in the direction of the Nigerian positions like a slightly more lethal version of a firework. With no guidance mechanism it was quite common for these rockets to go off track and even head back in the direction of the firing crew. The fact that the rockets could be as much of a danger to the firers as their intended targets is shown by a quote from a Nigerian officer, Lieutenant-Colonel Goodwin Ally, who said; 'You don't have to worry unless the thing lands on your head.'[18] Robert Walls, a photo journalist, wrote a very detailed description of the operating system of a rocket battery. Walls said;

> They consisted of three solid fuel rockets made from what appeared to be steel scaffolding pipe with fins welded to the back end. As I recall they were about 80cm long. Welded to the front were grenades and a flat steel bar on the launcher held the grenade handles in place. When readied for use the grenade pins were removed. The fuel was ignited by an electric spark by two wires through the cork in the back end. When the rockets took off up their launcher the grenade handles would slide clear of the retaining bar to arm the grenade which would explode at a fairly random height determined by the fuse.

An anti-aircraft version of the rocket could fly 5,000 yards but with no aiming mechanism hitting a MiG-17 would have been nothing short of a miracle.

Homemade Mortars

RAP technicians also tried to remedy the shortage of conventional artillery by producing their own mortars. They examined 3-inch and 2-inch mortars of Second World War vintage and tried to reverse engineer them. It was difficult to find suitable materials to make copies of the mortars, but they did manage to produce a few models. They were described as 'short range and low velocity' weapons and were used on several occasions by the Biafrans. One homemade mortar was reported to have been responsible for the first explosion in an action which destroyed a Federal convoy at Abagana in March 1968.

Other Weaponry

The Biafrans also came up with several other defensive weapons including the 'foot cutter,' which was made up of a drainpipe filled with shrapnel and scrap metal. This pipe had a u-bend at the top which was aimed towards oncoming Nigerian troops while an explosive charge was buried at its base. Often these smaller weapons were at ground level, hence the name of 'foot cutter' and were designed to disable the enemy rather than killing them outright. Another primitive weapon called the 'coffin' was basically a large rectangular shaped mine which was designed to be placed at the side of a main road. Its explosive charge was detonated via an electrical wire, sending scrap metal, ball bearings and broken glass into the

An infantry unit sorts its rifles and other small arms out and piles them rather clumsily in the centre of a village. The jumble of weapons includes a number of West German G-3 assault rifles and Second World War-era Mauser rifles. Two older soldiers are checking the weapons with one man holding a Bren Gun which appears to be this unit's only machinegun. Because of the shortage of weaponry in the Biafran Army the units armourers had to keep them in working order at all times. (Albert Grandolini Collection)

Nigerian columns. The Biafran workshops also produced a grenade based on the German 'potato-masher' of Second World War fame and was known as the 'Giraffe'. Other primitive Mills-type grenades were pictured being made in workshops by the RAP scientists. There were also reported to be attempts to produce a type of flamethrower, but this does not appear to have gone past the development stage.[19]

Shore Batteries

Biafran propaganda started the war suggesting that weaponry in its armouries were highly effective. In an attempt to counteract the lack of conventional weaponry they boasted about the 'ingenious' homemade weapons they had. These weapons took on almost 'supernatural' properties with the Biafran press failing to describe the weapons in detail. This was the case when it came to the 'shore batteries' which were successful in defending Onitsha from Nigerian river assaults in 1968. The average Biafran did not know what a 'shore battery' was, but they knew that it had killed hundreds or thousands of Nigerian troops. In reality, a shore battery was a collection of home-made mines, claymore type explosive launchers and rockets. When the Nigerians tried to cross the river to capture the opposite bank they were hit by machinegun and rifle fire. If they landed on the other bank they were hit by Ogbunigwes and other types of improvised weapons.

Military Transport

Motor transport in the Biafran Army was always in short supply with most units being lucky to have a single Land Rover or other improvised staff car available. At the start of the war there were reported to be about 200 trucks and 115 Land Rovers in military hands. This number was totally inadequate for the army's needs and the call went out for more vehicles. Civilian and commercial motor vehicles were confiscated by the military or sometimes donated by firms who were unable to get the scarce petrol to run them anyway. About 80 Land Rovers were requisitioned from the various government ministries and were taken to holding depots. Along with the other vehicles taken from various sources, the Land Rovers were inspected and serviced and then given a coat of camouflage paint. They were then given a stencilled registration, for instance 'BA 2050,' and the Biafran Army insignia on their mud guards. The intention was to share the available motor vehicles evenly amongst the various units, but this was not always the case. As with other scarce commodities in Biafra, it was often the case of first come first served and unit commanders would send their men to claim vehicles from the depots. Even in the early days there were not enough vehicles available and any kind of truck or car could be utilised. Peugeot 404 station wagons had been one of the most popular work vehicles for businesses in Nigeria before the war and now large numbers were used as staff cars. The famous 'mammy wagons,' which were gaudily painted trucks dating back to the 1940s, were also used in large numbers as transport vehicles. Before the war they had provided the main means of transport for ordinary people transporting goods and passengers to and from towns and markets. A boost to the transport problems came with the formation of the 'Civilian Transportation Corps'. This was a volunteer group made up of teachers, civil servants and taxi drivers who carried the wounded to hospital and military personnel to their units. Taxis were also requisitioned on a daily basis with their drivers supposedly paid for their services if they were lucky. As the war went on and spare parts began to run out many parts were made at Biafran metal shops. Although some parts could be produced there were other parts that could not be produced, such as head gaskets. Vehicles which had been driven on poor roads for many years began to break down at an alarming rate. Besides the lack of spare parts and the poor roads that vehicles had to travel on there was also the problem of poor drivers. The trucks and other vehicles had to be driven constantly in low gears which soon wore out their gear boxes. Some Biafran army drivers had little experience of driving and the crunching of gears and other bad habits put many vehicles off the road.

The shortage of fuel meant that some vehicles had to be taken off the road anyway and these were cannibalised for spare parts. Military units now often had to make do with one or two vehicles and overuse of these trucks and Land Rovers led to more breakdowns. Using various means, the Biafrans did manage to keep a skeleton force of transport vehicles on the road until the end of the war. Fuel shortages were an even more pressing issue even though the ingenious Biafrans built their own refineries. Every drop of petrol was precious, and civilians and the military tried to keep an emergency supply in case they needed to retreat from the Nigerians. Journalists were always shocked to see vehicles full of badly injured soldiers waiting patiently to be driven back to field hospitals. The reality was that the drivers were told not to take them until the vehicle was full and, in addition, it was better to drive at night to avoid the dreaded MiG-17s. For any soldier with a stomach wound or other internal injury this delay was a death sentence. Any internal wound that wasn't dealt with within a few hours would lead to death from septicaemia in the tropical heat. The shortage of vehicles as the war progressed led to units stealing each other's cars and trucks. There were also a lot of vehicles moving around Biafra that belonged to aid organisations like Caritas and the Red Cross. On several occasions European mercenaries decided to confiscate these vehicles, including several Swedish Volvo Laplander off road cars. These were stolen by officers of the 4th Commando Division resulting in their expulsion from Biafra by Colonel Ojukwu. Communications between units was commonly reliant upon motorcycle messengers who carried messages and often used jungle tracks in order to avoid the Nigerians who were using the main roads. The main types of motorcycle in use with the Biafrans were Hondas from 90cc and 250cc and nearly all had been requisitioned from their civilian owners. Bicycles were widely used by the Biafran population in general and were often piled high with both passengers and goods. The Biafran army also used bicycles to transport their men to the front and they were utilised in several 'behind the lines' operations. Bicycle troops were able to move easily along poor jungle tracks and this allowed them to move around Federal fixed positions and communication lines which were usually tied to the main roads. As with everything else in Biafra, however, bicycles and their spare parts were often in short supply and the majority of the army had to rely on their own legs to get from a to b. Keeping military vehicles on the road was always a problem for the Biafran Army, especially when it came to providing fuel for them. The ingenuity of the Biafran scientists extended to producing petrol and other fuels in a number of large and small refineries. Several large refineries were able to produce 20,000 gallons of fuel per day to keep the Biafran Army's depleting fleet of trucks, Land Rovers and cars on the road. The refineries were built in jungle bases and were heavily camouflaged against air raids. Larger units had their own small-scale refineries to provide the fuel needs for their vehicles. These refineries were producing an average of 500 gallons of fuel per day which was sufficient to keep a few vehicles on the road.

Chapter 5
Combat Operations of the Biafran War

From the declaration of the secession of Biafra from Nigeria in late May 1967 until July of that year a 'phoney war' existed. Neither side wanted to make the first military moves as both the Nigerian Federal Army and the Biafran Army desperately tried to prepare for war. The chronology of the Nigerian Civil War can be divided into five distinct phases from July 1967 until January 1970. During the first phase, from July to August 1967, the Nigerian and Biafran Armies began by launching probing patrols into each other's territory. Nigeria saw this first phase as a 'police action against a rebel clique' and tried to defeat the Biafrans without having to mount a full-scale war. The police action only lasted a few weeks before Nigerian units began to advance into Biafra and took the university city of Nsukku. The Biafrans then launched their surprise invasion of the unguarded Mid-West region by a cobbled together force of 1,000 men in August. Even though the invasion force was small and poorly armed it still employed a large part of Biafra's paltry resources. When it failed, in September, the Biafrans had lost their only real chance of winning the war or gaining independence.

A longer, second phase of the war lasted from August 1967 until October 1968, and saw full-scale offensive operations by the Nigerian armed forces. This was the most disastrous period for the Biafrans, who lost not only their capital Enugu, and the major city Onitsha, but also the ports of Calabar and Port Harcourt. Indeed, the rebels almost capitulated as the territory under their control shrunk drastically.

The third phase went from October 1968 to April 1969 and saw a revival by the Biafrans thanks to arms deliveries from France, and the creation of a new air force equipped with light strikers. Certainly enough, Biafra lost its second wartime capital, Owerri, and its population began suffering mass starvation, but it continued fighting.

The fourth phase lasted from April 1969 to November 1969: it saw the loss of the Biafra's third wartime capital of Umuahia, but also the liberation of Owerri. War weariness now took hold of both parties and a military stalemate developed before the situation worsened for the Biafams once again, in November 1969, starting the fifth and final phase of the war, which was to last until January 1970.

Initial Operations: July-September 1967

The small Biafran Army of a few thousand troops had about a month to prepare for war against the 6,000 strong Nigerian Army. Right from the beginning, the Biafran insistence on taking on their enemy in conventional warfare put their armed forces at a severe disadvantage. Colonel Ojukwu with his Sandhurst military education was adamant that guerrilla warfare was to be avoided. His officers coming from the same background generally had the same narrow-minded attitude to the coming war. The effect on them and especially on the soldiers they commanded was summed up by Michael Gould:

> This was a war fought with modern armament and technology, and controlled and led on both sides by Sandhurst and Mons trained men, who had all been comrades in a very close-knit community, the Nigerian Army. They had all been taught all aspects of conducting military campaigns as learnt and perceived by European and Western societies. However the war was contested by ill-educated and generally illiterate people who had little understanding of the modern independent state of Nigeria, let alone a war fought in European style with fairly up-to-date equipment....[1]

When the fighting began, there were only two regular Biafran battalions available and these were stationed on the Northern

Casualties are brought to the rear by canoe during the June 1968 fighting for the town of Afam. Although this was not the most ideal method of transported wounded it was still preferable to the alternative of being carried on makeshift stretchers often for several days. Some of the soldiers have simple uniforms while the others are wearing the civilian clothing they went to the front in. (Author's Collection)

In this photograph by Romano Cagnoni which sums up the sheer terror of combat a group of Biafran soldiers rush their badly wounded comrade away from the fighting. The wounded soldier clutches his stomach in agony having taken a bullet or shrapnel to that part of the body. His chances of survival would have been slim as he would have been fortunate to get transport to a field hospital and may have lain waiting for treatment for hours or even days. (Romano Cagnoni)

Front. They were totally unprepared to face the large Nigerian Army, with few weapons apart from small arms and machineguns. Unsurprisingly, it was an almost pointless attempt and the Biafrans thus concentrated on buying time until the promised arms arrived. They thus withdrew from Nsukku in the north, bolstering the Nigerian impression that the Biafrans were poor combatants. One report stressed that a Nigerian unit at Obudu advancing on a Biafran position came under fire while still well out of range. It stated; 'The Ibos started shooting when the patrol was a mile and a half away,' and continued with commentary that while the Biafrans claimed to have killed 35 Federal troops, they actually withdrew before the Nigerians came close enough to be shot.[2]

As well as a lack of arms, the Biafrans were handicapped by the lack of communication equipment, which made it impossible for their commanders to coordinate their forces and operations. Moreover, although the defenders had done their best to prepare defensive positions there were simply too few troops to man them. For example, the defences in the south were in the hands of hastily raised militia and civilians armed with machetes, a few shotguns and dane guns. The few fortifications constructed for the defence of Port Harcourt were well-built but too few in numbers, while the sole 105mm field gun was moved from place to place in attempt to counter the Nigerian attacks but only a few shells were available at any time, and was thus almost useless.

Operation Torch: Invasion of the Mid-West

In an audacious attempt to draw away Nigerian forces from their campaign in the north of Biafra, Ojukwu and his aides set up an invasion of the Mid-West region. Their plan was to deploy a mechanised force of about 100 vehicles packing about 1,000 troops – dubbed the '101st Division' – to quickly cross the Niger River that formed the 'border' with Nigeria, and advance as far as possible. The vehicles assembled for this operation by Colonel Victor Banjo (a Mid-Westerner from the Yoruba tribe), were made up of commandeered 'mammy wagons', private cars, station wagons, and vans, and Land Rovers of the police and the army. Some of the Land Rovers had been hastily armoured with metal plate or corrugated iron sheeting and the whole column must have had a motley appearance. Banjo's involvement was hoped to attract additional officers and troops to the Biafran side. In reality, Colonel Banjo was a confident and ambitious officer with his own – secret – agenda, which was nothing less than a 'liberation' of all of southern Nigeria, and thus grabbing power from Gowon.

Operation Torch was initiated on 9 August 1967, at 0300 in the morning, when the column – organised into three similar-sized battalions, the 12th, 13th, and 18th, equipped with the only heavy weaponry and machineguns the Biafrans had – crossed the Onitsha Bridge and motored at speed through Mid-West State. With the mass of the Nigerian Army deployed on the Northern Front, the Federals were capable of assembling only a few hundred men to oppose Banjo's force: even then, these consisted of administrative staff, Gowon's personal bodyguards, and police officers. Moreover, about 28 officers of ethnic Ibo background defected to the rebel side.

However, the command structure of the 101st Division was in such disarray that the volunteers that joined them while underway made no difference: the column moved slowly, stopping at various

A Biafran Sergeant adjusts the sights on his Spanish Type L 81mm mortar to make sure he doesn't waste any of his scarce bombs. Several of this model of mortar were seen in service with the Biafrans and were probably bought from a private arms dealer. There is no record of the Spanish Government selling this type of weapon to the Biafrans directly. (Private Collection)

Smartly turned out soldiers of the 12th Division which was formed in January 1968 from amongst all available units in the Calabar, Uyo and Eket provinces. The two soldiers guard a government building armed with two different Czech weapons, the vz. 58 assault rifle and a M23 sub-machinegun. (Via Albert Grandolini)

Standing guard over a government building this well-dressed machinegun crew are armed with a Czechoslovakian Zb Model 53 mounted in the back of a Land Rover. Few Biafran soldiers would have been lucky enough to attain this level of uniformity and these men obviously belong to an elite unit. The soldier sat on the right of the photograph is also armed with a Czechoslovakian CZ-247 sub-machinegun one of several types imported from that country. (Robert Walls)

points for days. The first aim of the operation, Benin City (the capital of Mid-West State), was captured during the first afternoon of the offensive. Rather than exploiting the moment of surprise, the Biafrans then settled in the town: Banjo wasted time by trying to contact any military- and civilian official he could, while his troops looted £14 million from local banks: only about £2 million were sent to Biafra, the rest went missing.

Banjo next declared the 'Republic of Benin', and was promptly appointed a military governor by Ojukwu – although, reportedly, meanwhile plotting a coup against the Biafran leader. Moreover, the heavy-handed treatment of non-Ibo people quickly lost the Biafrans all potential allies and they converted into a disorganised occupation force. It was thus only on 17 August 1967 that the Biafrans continued their advance and crossed into the West State, heading for Lagos. On the next day, they reached Ore. By this time, every available Nigerian soldier – 'including cooks and bottle washers' – had been drafted into the force assembled to stop them. Moreover, as the 101st attempted to continue its advance, it found that the bridges to the west and north had all been blown up. The advance thus petered out in a series of skirmishes in the Ore area, fought between 20 and 28 August. Although the Nigerian Army was able to muster only about 1,500 troops, these decided the fate of the entire country: the Biafran advance lost its momentum and Banjo's troops lost their will to fight. Before long, the commander of the 101st became obsessed with being outflanked by the reported concentration of Nigerian troops.

Indeed, the Nigerians finally got their act together and recruited a divisional-size unit to recover the Mid-West. The resulting 2nd Division was actually staffed by poorly trained recruits, however it launched its counteroffensive on 9 September, moving in three columns supported by armoured cars and artillery. Realising that the big gamble had failed, Banjo ordered a withdrawal of the 101st Division from Benin on 12 September. Furious about this failure, on 19 September 1967 Ojukwu ordered his commander back to Enugu to explain himself. As he was driving with his entourage back to the Biafran capital his men were in the middle of their slow and disorganised retreat back through West and Mid-West states. During their withdrawal, the Biafrans vented their frustrations on any non-Ibo civilians, committing numerous atrocities. Benin thus fell on 20 September 1967, without much fighting.

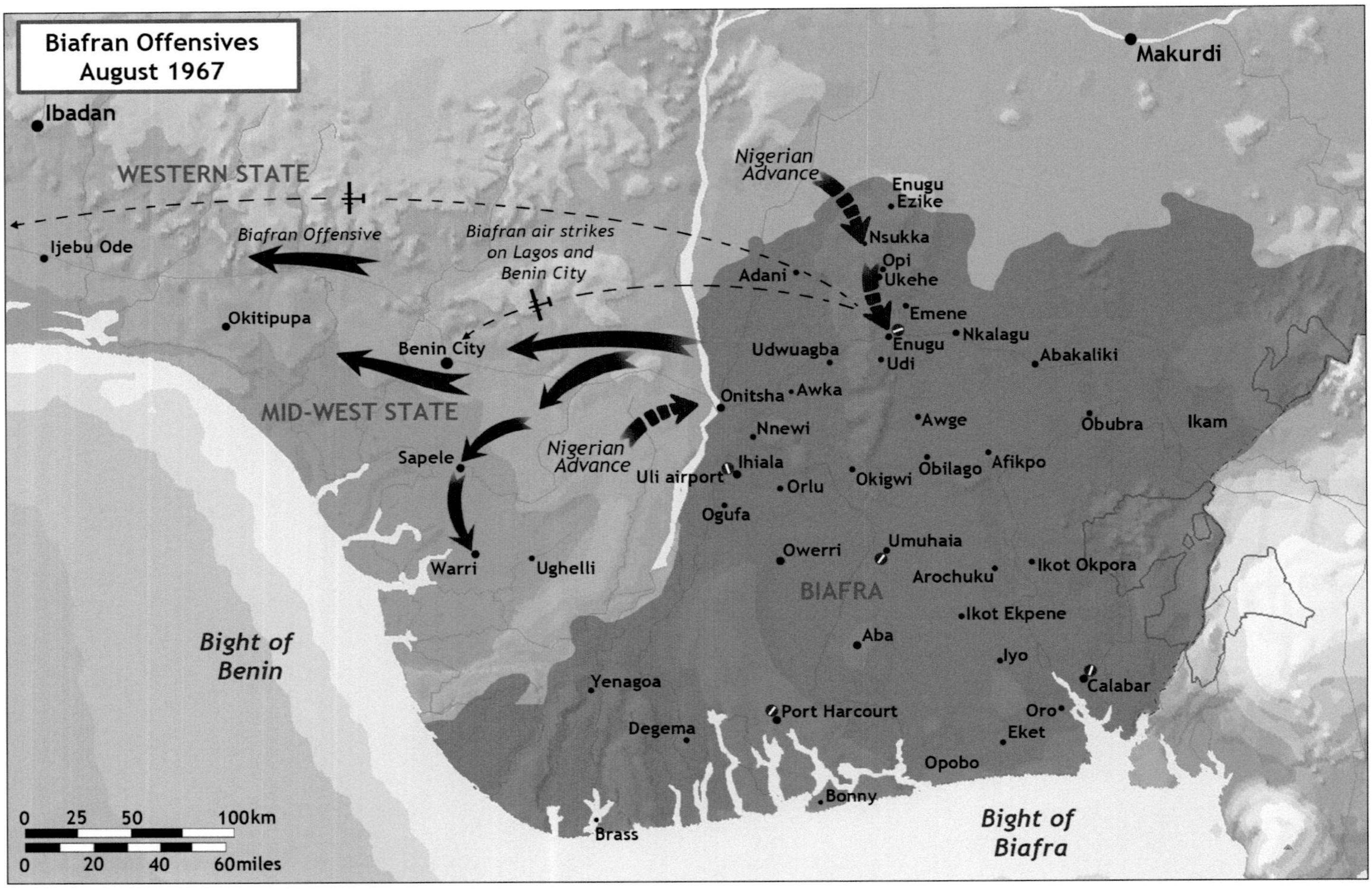

Opening moves of both the Nigerian Army (segmented arrows) and the Biafran Army (solid arrows) between may and December 1967. The map also shows air raids flown by the Biafran Air Force during the summer and early autumn of the same year. (Map by Tom Cooper)

This photograph taken in August 1968 shows a unit of Biafran troops leaving their trench to attack Nigerian trenches only 100 yards away. The troops are trying to defend the city of Aba from the advancing Federal Army but the city finally fell on 4 September. Colonel Steiner's 4th Commando Division had been heavily involved in the defence of Aba and had suffered heavy casualties. (Author's Collection)

Once back in Enugu, Banjo, Lieutenant-Colonel Emmanuel Ifeajuna, Majors Alele and Sam Agham were promptly arrested and put on trial by a hastily convened 'kangaroo court'. Accused of withdrawing without Ojukwu's permission and plotting to overthrow the Biafran leader, they were all found guilty, taken out and quickly shot. Meanwhile, Ojukwu also went as far as to dismiss his Commander-in-Chief, Colonel Njoku, and replace him with Colonel Madeibo. The withdrawal of the 101st Division was stopped only once its last troops crossed back to Biafran territory on 6 October 1967, blowing up two spans of the bridge before the Federals could advance across it.

The War in the South

Before the Biafran invasion of the Mid-West got underway an equally important battle was going on in the south. The newly organised Nigerian 3rd Division launched an amphibious assault on the Island of Bonny at the mouth of the important Port Harcourt harbour on 17 July. A 1,000-man assault force carried in two Federal Navy ships was landed on Bonny Island pushing aside the small company-sized Biafran defence force. The taking of Bonny sealed off Port Harcourt and the oil terminals and

Two Biafran soldiers move forward at the double towards Nigerian positions during fighting near Aba in August 1968. Although both men have steel helmets the man in the foreground is wearing a US M1 model while his comrade has a locally made helmet. These construction worker type helmets were made in Biafran workshops from forming metal plate over a wooden mould. Often the metal from milk tins supplied as part of the food relief was used to make the helmets but they provided no protection at all for the wearer. (Private Collection)

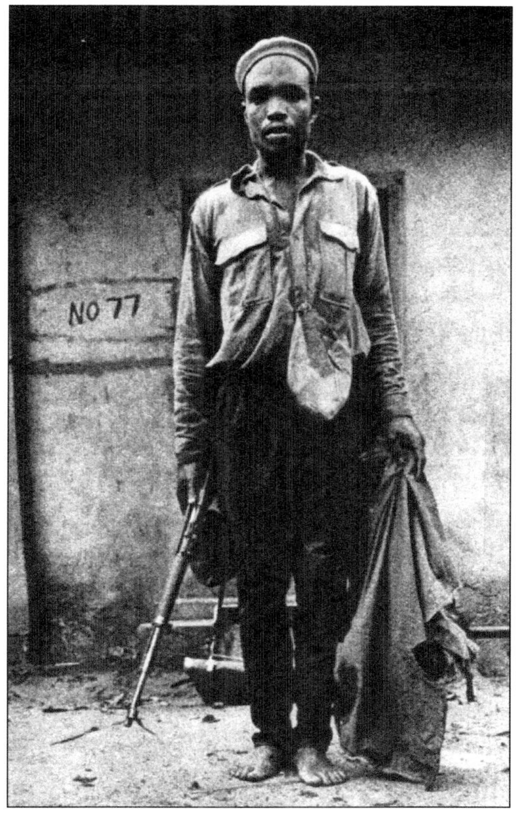

Biafran Army Corporal Ogbonna Okolie Stands in front of the boots of a fallen Nigerian soldier to pay his foe due respect before putting them on in August 1968. He told the photographer his name and said: "I shot one of the vandals. There were two climbing down from trees. One turned his gun on me. I shot him in the belly. The other disappeared". Although he showed no regret about the killing he wanted to show the dead Nigerian soldier that he did have respect for him as a fellow warrior. (Private Collection)

Biafran troops surround a terrified 18-year-old Nigerian prisoner who has only been in the army for two months. He is very lucky to be alive as few prisoners were taken by either side in this bitter conflict. His captors are dressed in the usual array of military and quasi-military uniforms with most wearing the Biafran type field cap while two have acquired steel helmets. Rifles are from left to right, an H&K G3 assault rifle, vz. 58 assault rifle and a Mauser 98k type bolt action rifle which could have come from numerous sources. (Richard Hall)

began the Nigerian blockade of the Biafran coastline. Most foreign commentators agreed that the Biafrans could not survive for long without a way to breach this blockade.

Fighting for Onitsha

After chasing the Biafrans back across the Niger River the recently formed 2nd Division of the Nigerian Army found itself deployed opposite Onitsha. For a while the wide river would act as an obstacle, at least until the Nigerians found a way to cross. The first assault on Onitsha was launched in early October 1967, by when the local Baifran garrison was still made up of only three weak battalions: the 11th, 12th, and 18th. Although defended by only about 1,200 poorly-armed men – mostly survivors of Operation Torch – this attack was thrown back, after heavy fighting on the streets of

In this action photograph taken in August 1968, the officer on the right urges his reluctant soldier forward and tells him to get to his feet. The reporter said that he shouted "On your feet you coward" and when this didn't work he shot at the terrified soldier's feet. Realising he had little choice the soldier got up and followed his commander fearing his anger as much as the enemy's bullets. (Private Collection)

Poorly armed and wearing little or no uniform these young soldiers, including a 13-year-old at the rear, move cautiously towards Nigerian lines. They are all armed with Lee Enfield .303 rifles which had the nickname 'chaka-ko' or 'cock and shoot' amongst Biafran soldiers. Some soldiers used bayonets with this rifle and were told by their instructors that they contained poison. (Romano Cagnoni)

This young soldier is under the command of Lieutenant-Colonel Ogbonnaga Oji, the 32-year-old officer who personally led his men into battle in August 1968. According to the reporter his men included soldiers as young as 15 who shouted the battle cry "War! Win! War! Win!" The soldier wears a well-worn field cap and has the ubiquitous rising sun patch on his short sleeve. (Author's Collection)

Colonel Ojukwu gives the visiting press a summary of the war situation in the summer of 1968. The Biafran leader had a calm and reassured manner about him even in the darkest days of 1968. He had extra pressure on him as so many of the Biafran population truly believed that he could lead them to victory despite all the odds against them. Ojukwu allowed far more access to the international press than his counterpart General Gowon. (Author's Collection)

Onitsha with hundreds of casualties, on 9 October. This success became possible foremost because the Biafrans sunk dozens of assault boats – including one by a homemade rocket fired in the general direction of the Nigerians.

After licking their wounds, regrouping and refitting, the Nigerians launched their second attempt on 20 October 1967: once again, this was defeated with the help of homemade weapons – just like the third assault, launched in late November. By then, the Nigerian Army suffered an estimated 1,000 casualties in this campaign, for no gain at all: time and again, it would manage to get its troops across the river, but these always failed to establish a bridgehead. For the time being, Onitsha was thus safe and the two sides settled down for months of stalemate on this frontline.

The fall of Enugu

While the offensive on Onitsha went nowhere, the Federal 1st Division advanced from the north to the Biafran capital Enugu. The local terrain and the lack of weaponry and troops forced the

The wrecks of several trucks lie on the road at Abagana, the scene of the ambush and destruction of a Nigerian supply column of the 2nd Division on its way to Onitsha. Although the official Biafran version is that the last mortar round of their unit set off a chain reaction of explosions along the column it may have been that it was in fact a series of small attacks on groups of trucks. (Albert Grandolini Collection)

Biafrans to evacuate most of the population, the government and all of its civil servants, and the Nigerians reached the outskirts by 1 October 1967. Certainly enough, the local leaders managed to raise a militia of about 10,000 volunteers and whipped them up into a patriotic frenzy in a series of speeches: however, the troops in question were only armed with machetes and a few shotguns, and – after being bussed in the direction of the enemy – were quickly dispersed by Nigerian artillery, mortars and armoured cars. Although fighting for Enugu continued for a few days it only resulted in the deaths of 30 young Biafran officers and a few dozen soldiers. By 4 October 1967, all of the Biafran troops had withdrawn to the south and the Biafran capital had been occupied by the Nigerians.

Disarray of late 1967 and early 1968

In the aftermath of the fall of Nsukku and Enugu, and the defeat of the Mid-West invasion, the Biafran Army was in total disarray. There was really only the 52nd Brigade in the south capable of putting up a fight. The 51st and 53rd Brigades were in chaos and there were about 4,000 Biafran troops virtually roaming around the countryside. Remnants of the Mid-West invasion force were joined with other homeless troops to form three weak Battalions, the 11th, 12th and 18th, each with about 400 men. Other estimates of the strength of the army after the fall of Nsukku put it at 7,000, but there was no doubt that most of the troops were totally despondent in the wake of the unexpected defeats they had suffered.

A recovery of sorts saw the army expand to about 25,000 men in early 1968, but many of these were unarmed. In reality, the total number of Biafran troops did not really matter, as only those armed counted. Moreover, by early 1968 the Biafrans were no longer using their surviving armoured vehicles apart from those captured from the Nigerians in battle. Other than the odd artillery piece and mortar the Biafrans were usually facing their well-armed enemy with little more than bolt action rifles: it was also suffering from chronic shortages of ammunition. By August 1968 the army was losing up to 100 men per day, and before French arms arrived it still had fewer than 50 percent of its nominal troops armed.

Fall of Onitsha

The valiant Biafran defence of Onitsha in late 1967 had cost the Nigerian 2nd Division dearly. However, this success could not be sustained for very long. After – finally – realising that he had to expect fierce resistance, the commander of the 2nd Division, Lieutenant-Colonel Murtala Mohammed, decided to cross the Niger River north of the city, instead of launching another frontal assault. This time, his units not only took the Biafrans by surprise: the garrison of Onitsha had too few troops and arms to protect a wider front. The 2nd Division thus advanced around the town and attacked it from the direction of Akwa. This time the defences collapsed quickly and Ontisha fell on 22 March 1968.

By this time, out of its pre-war population of 160,000, only 715 people were left in the town: most of the fleeing civilians had joined the growing throng of refugees meanwhile moving towards the centre of the remaining Biafran territory. Worse yet, during this retreat, the last Biafran Army unit still protecting the area of the Niger bridge ran into a Nigerian ambush while withdrawing and lost 270 men killed on 23 March 1968. A day later, the Biafran troops still in the outskirts of Onitsha launched a futile counterattack, only to find themselves hopelessly outnumbered by the Nigerians.

Having secured the town, the Nigerian forces settled down into an uncomfortable occupation of the deserted city, isolated and dependent on long and fragile supply lines.

Abagana Ambush

Although Ojukwu and his officers refused to deploy their troops in a guerrilla war, they still found a way to interdict the supply line of the 2nd Division. In late March 1968, they were informed about a convoy of 96 trucks full of supplies, ammunition and fuel, protected by just one Saladin and two Ferret armoured cars, that was about to travel from Abagana for Onitsha. Under cover of the surrounding jungle, the Biafran troops commanded by Major Uchenda set up an ambush on 31 March 1968: they let the lead Saladin pass by before simultaneously opening fire from several points along the full length of the column. Once the leading lorry was knocked out, the rest of the column became 'sitting ducks', unable to run or hide. According to eyewitnesses, a lucky shot by a Biafran mortar crew hit one of the tankers whose fuel then engulfed much of the convoy. Other sources say that the homemade mortar which had a primitive aiming system used its last bomb in the attack. The Nigerians tried to launch a counterattack from the rear of the column, but this was quickly beaten back. An hour long fire fight then ensued during which the Federal troops lost one of their Ferrets to the Biafrans. Most of the Nigerian truck drivers and guards had been gunned down, but their trucks were alight and only a fraction of their precious cargo was saved from the flames. As was usual whenever

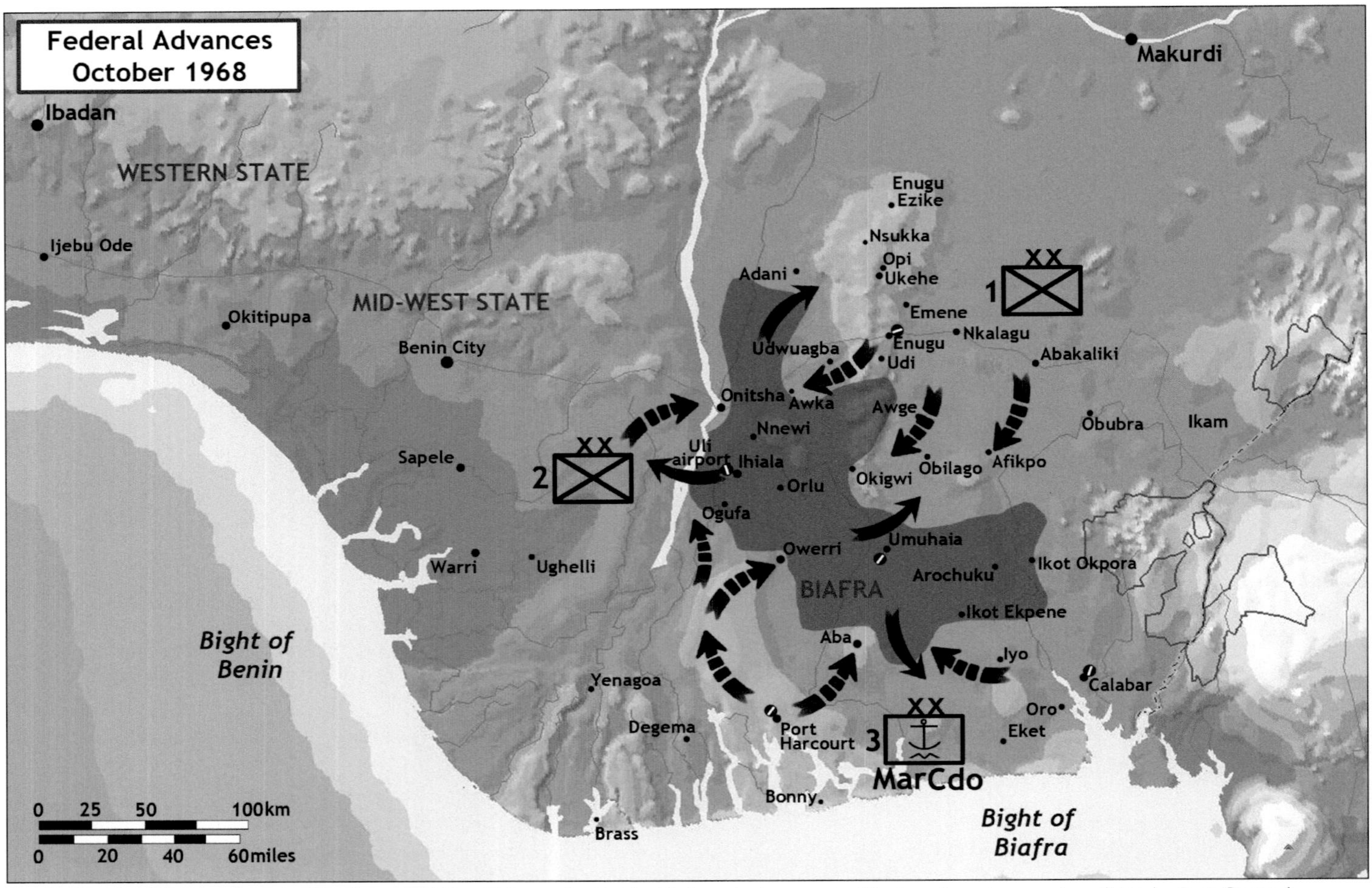

A map showing Nigerian Army's offensives of 1968, which resulted in the Biafrans losing most of their major urban centres. (Map by Tom Cooper)

they scored one of their rare military victories in this war, the Biafran propaganda agency Markpress exploited this opportunity to the utmost to boost the morale of the population at home, but also amongst sympathisers abroad.

Fall of Port Harcourt

Port Harcourt was one of the most important cities in pre-war Nigeria, serving as a major linchpin to the entire world. Its importance for Biafra and its war effort cannot be overstated. Unsurprisingly, the rebels took great care to heavily fortify the approaches to it by early 1968, especially so south of the city, which at the start of the war had a population of about 360,000. The closest positions of the Nigerian Army were in Bonny, about 25 miles down the road over difficult terrain, full of creeks and mangroves: actually, the best way to reach Port Harcourt was along the Bonny River in the Niger Delta, which ran through both cities. Still, this crucial port was de-facto under a siege by 17 January 1968, even though life largely went on as normal. It was only in late January that the Federal army claimed to have reached the suburbs. However, such reports proved unreliable: the Biafrans were able to stop the tentative advances of the 3rd Marine-Commando Division in a series of skirmishes. The fighting then ebbed and flowed for several months, with both sides claiming to have taken prisoners and captured arms from each other. Indeed, through March and April, Nigerian overclaiming only continued by playing into the hands of the Biafrans. However, by 16 May 1968, the continuous build-up of the Nigerian forces around Port Harcourt – followed by flanking movements that cut the two main road connections to the north – meant that the city was virtually surrounded and besieged.

Initially at least, the commander of the 3rd Marine-Commando Division, Colonel Adekunle, had left the roads open to allow civilians to escape, hoping that they would foul up the Biafran defences. Over the following days, up to 80% of the population escaped, leaving most of Port Harcourt deserted. Then, on 18 May, Adekunle launched his assault, and – at least officially – the crucial port fell to the 3rd Marine-Commando Division on the following day. However, only a day later, the Biafrans launched a major counterattack, provoking an extensive battle for the local airport: the fighting then went on for several weeks as about 2,000 Biafran soldiers were trapped inside and looking for a way out. Adekunle gloated about his victory and said that the only way out would be by, 'jumping in the water'. Eventually, it was only on 9 June 1968 that the last defenders were overpowered. Even after that date, some Biafran units remained in the surrounding bush.[3]

Operation OAU

July 1968 saw the Biafrans encircled in an enclave of 3,000 square miles. This much-reduced area now contained only three major urban centres: Aba, Owerri and Umuahia. Peace talks were meanwhile organised in the north-western African state of Niger, and in Addis Ababa, the Ethiopian capital, during which the intensity of the fighting slackened. Colonel Adekunle exploited this opportunity to prepare his 3rd Division for its next major offensive: Operation OAU – the main objective of which was the capture of Owerri, and the secondary the town of Aba. The offensive was led by 16th Brigade, which advanced in the centre: the 14th followed on the right flank in the direction of Aba, while the 15th was to support the assault on Oweri and then to advance on the river town of Oguta. Two further brigades – the 13th and the 18th – were kept back as reserve.

Captain Emmanuel Nwobosi who was serving as Ojukwu's Chief of Staff in 1969 is seen on a tour of inspection. Nwobosi was involved in the January 1966 coup and went on to join the Biafran Army at the start of the civil war. He was seen as an expert in guerrilla warfare but was wounded in action so was transferred to Army HQ. (Author's Collection)

These enthusiastic dancing soldiers have been newly recruited into the Biafran 14th Division in late March 1969. According to the photograph caption they have been drafted into the army rather than volunteering. Many arrived at the recruiting station in a poor physical condition prompting their officers to demand: "Get a better lot by tomorrow morning!" This group shouting "Death to the Nigerians, Victory to Biafra!" may have to go into battle soon without rifles due to local shortages. (Author's Collection)

Operation OAU was initiated on 4 September: Aba duly fell, followed by Owerri on 16th of the same month. Desperate attempts of the Biafran 4th Commando Brigade and a few other, scattered units (about 2,000 troops in total), were all easily repelled by the vastly superior Nigerians. Indeed, after securing his two initial objectives, Adekunle pushed his 3rd Division on to Umhuahia – his final objective – with which he was literally obsessed. However, this move left the – now much weakened – 16th Brigade that garrisoned Oweri isolated from allied units. Moreover, undertaken in a great rush, the assault on Umhuahia was poorly organised, and run as the 3rd Division began to run out of steam, while encountering bitter resistance. The result was unavoidable: although 15th Brigade had managed to secure Oguta, thus reaching an area only 12 miles from Uli airfield (whose fall could have ended the war at that point in time), the Nigerians were forced to withdraw. Indeed, realising the seriousness of the situation, Ojukwu deployed all of the available units in this direction, and these chased 15th Brigade not only out of Oguta, but also away from numerous oilfields – the recovery of which saved an already fatally weakened Biafran Army.

Struggle for Ikot-Ekpene

Ikot-Ekpene was one of the most strategically important towns for the Biafrans both as a road junction and because it was positioned on the southern boundary of Biafran held territory for much of the war. From early 1968 it was under threat from the 3rd Division's advance from the Calabar area. The town fell first to the Nigerians during heavy fighting which lasted from 29 March until 12 April, when the Nigerian Air Force (NAF) softened up the Biafran defences with one of its first major air raids. However, when the Federal troops finally entered the town, they were surprised to find it defended by just 30 regular Biafran troops and a few militiamen.

Soldiers of the Biafran 14th Division are seen after a skirmish with Federal troops on the outskirts of Owerri. They wear the usual mixture of uniform items taken from whatever source and the NCO in the foreground appears to be wearing civilian clothing with military insignia added. The boy soldier behind him has put a metal pot on his head for protection as they move towards the frontline. (Daniel Camus)

A young Biafran soldier looks nervously towards enemy positions before beginning to move down a jungle road in 1969. He has the peak of his classic Biafran field cap pushed up at the front and wears it along with a complete uniform of jungle green shirt and trousers. Worn on his waist belt he has the bayonet for his vz. 58 assault rifle and also has a canvas haversack to carry spare magazines. (Romano Cagnoni)

In this image the soldier in the previous photograph is joined by another young soldier who appears to be dressed identically. His comrade has the Czech Army issue magazine holder which is curved to accommodate the 30 round magazine of the vz. 58. The first soldier's kit can be seen more clearly in this photograph and his belt has pouches with tools in them to maintain his assault rifle. (Romano Cagnoni)

The first attempt to recover Ikot-Ekpene was launched by the Biafrans in mid-April 1968: they failed to break through though and found themselves encamped in the outskirts. Ojukwu then ordered the 12th Division to the scene and to recover the town at any cost. Attacking in force, the Biafrans managed to push the Nigerians out by five miles, and even to capture an artillery base together with a significant amount of arms and ammunition, including 100,000 bullets, 300 shells for 105mm artillery, two anti-aircraft guns, 50 motorcycles, three battery-charging machines, four wireless sets, and three typewriters.

General Effiong now argued that his hometown should be heavily defended, 'but only for strategic reasons.' Colonel Ojukwu replied sarcastically that perhaps his hometown – Nnewi – should also be heavily defended for the same reason. Whatever was the case, the Biafran forces managed to retain control over Ikot-Ekpene for several months longer, despite constant pressure by the Nigerians. Receiving little sympathy from either side, the civilian population suffered terribly: indeed, the Biafran Army put most of the blame for civilian casualties upon 'activities of disloyal minorities.' The fighting went on without disruption and the 3rd Marine-Commando Division retook Ikot-Ekpene in early September 1968 – only to lose it again by the end of the same month.

In a typical scene of the civil war a small unit of Biafran troops have emerged from the jungle to overwhelm a patrol of Federal troops. Once the enemy have been captured they have been stripped of all weapons, uniforms and equipment which would be shared out amongst their captors. Such small victories were celebrated by the Biafrans mainly because of the 'war booty' they gained from them. (Author's Collection)

Two soldiers dressed in rags pose in front of their comrades who had just ambushed a unit of Federal troops close to the city of Aba. Even when they were issued with uniforms Biafran soldiers would be lucky to get replacements once theirs had worn out. Civilian clothing usually had to be worn alongside military items to complete a quasi-military uniform for many Biafrans. One commentator said that solders wore "disintegrating battledress and bright civvy shirts". (Private Collection)

The Biafran Army in late 1968 and early 1969

In late October 1968 Colonel Ojukwu claimed that he could easily raise an army several times the size of the present Biafran Army;

Troops are not the problem: if I want 100,000 men I only have

This sergeant of the 'S' Division urges his men to attack as they come under fire from the Nigerians on the outskirts of Owerri. He has the usual Biafran sun emblem on his upper sleeve and the red lightning flash on black patch of the 'S' Division below it. His rifle is an H&K G3 assault rifle which was issued usually to the shock platoon of a Biafran unit. Tragically this young NCO was killed in action the very next day according to Romano Cagnoni the photographer. (Romano Cagnoni)

Biafran soldiers seen just after they have successfully ambushed a Nigerian patrol in the summer of 1969. The victorious troops have already stripped their terrified captives of their uniforms and precious equipment. As well as the shirts, trousers and boots the webbing was also prized as many Biafran troops had to carry spare ammunition in their pockets. Often the better dressed rebel troops would be those who were daring enough to launch these types of ambush to gain their 'war booty'. (Private Collection)

During the fighting for Owerri a light mortar crew fire towards Nigerian positions protected by a comrade carrying a French WW2 MAS-36 rifle. In the confused fighting fought in dense undergrowth the enemy could be less than a 100 yards away. Any hits on the Federal Army position would usually be met by return fire from their artillery or mortars. In most cases the number of shells that were fired back by the Nigerians would be many times those fired by the Biafrans. (Albert Grandolini Collection)

This scene from the summer fighting of 1969 shows an advancing column of troops armed mostly with Mauser rifles. They are moving towards the smoke from a burning village which they are contesting in one of the many local battles of the war. The war was made up of a large number of small battles and skirmishes for control of villages and several large battles for the larger towns and cities of Biafra. (Albert Grandolini Collection)

> to say the word and in 72 hours I will have them… the problem is arming them. If I have the weapons, I could possibly put three times the force now in operation in the field.[4]

Indeed, heavy losses – most of these caused by the lack of arms, ammunition and generally poor organisation and leadership of the Biafran armed forces – kept the average strength of his army at 40,000 men for most of 1968. It was only in summer of that year that the arrival of additional arms and ammunition enabled Ojukwu to put more men under arms. Even then, and although the flow of arms then continued almost undisrupted, further expansion was rather gradual, and the army grew to only about 70,000 by early 1969. The reason was that additional troops required far more supplies than were available: thus, although about 30,000 additional, lightly armed troops were on hand, they were not deployed as regulars, but as mere 'cannon fodder'. The latter was a particularly important factor because the Biafrans were meanwhile forced to change their strategy: while they would often quickly withdraw from any threatened towns or villages at earlier times, there was now no space left to withdraw to. The Biafrans were fighting for their naked survival. Moreover, thanks to the French deliveries of arms, their morale was improved significantly. Taffy Williams – now one of only four mercenaries confirmed as still in Biafra – explained: 'It was more a matter of psychology than any new supply of weapons. The army really pulled its socks up and its soldiers simply decided they weren't going to retreat anymore.'[5]

Early 1969

The extensive fighting of the summer and autumn 1968 exhausted both sides, and a four-month stalemate – combined with a Christmas truce – ensued, lasting well into late January 1969, providing both sides with a welcome respite. While one might expect that this was of major advantage for the Federal troops in particular, the result was quite to the contrary: the 2nd Division of the Nigerian Army meanwhile not only proved unable to continue its advance from Ontisha, but also suffered from poor morale as a result of subsequent inaction. Adekunle's 3rd Division was meanwhile tied down in

Biafran soldiers bring in a trussed Nigerian prisoner into to their jungle Headquarters to be interrogated. He has been stripped down to his underwear and his precious uniform and equipment shared out amongst his captors. Prisoners were not always taken by either side in the civil war and this man has escaped summary justice in the bush. Unless he is an officer they will gain little information from him as ordinary soldiers, as in most wars, knew little outside their immediate surroundings. (Romano Cagnoni)

By 1969 when this photograph was taken the already small number of motor vehicles available to the Biafran Army had shrunk drastically. Lorries had to be cannibalised to keep others on the road and even the ingenious Biafrans could not keep totally worn out vehicles going for ever. The crew of this truck have pulled it into a roadside covered area and put palm fronds on the front to camouflage it. (Author's Collection)

the Owerri area and hit by renewed counterattacks every time it attempted to continue its advance. Finally, the Nigerian offensive in the Abagana sector of the new Biafran capital of Umhuahia, was making next to no progress. Unsurprisingly, the commanders in Lagos soon concluded that there was a serious incentive to continue the advance into the Ibo-heartland, regardless of what kind of resistance was awaiting them there. This is how the idea came into being for the – much vaunted – 'Final Offensive.'

By that point in the war, the NAF and its MiG-17s had not proven to be particularly effective. However, in early 1969, they escalated their campaign of air strikes, targeting civilian facilities and military positions alike in an attempt to 'soften up' the Biafrans before the ground assault. During January and February, the MiG-17s of the NAF concentrated most of their air strikes on the Umhuahia area: by March, they had been joined by a handful of Ilyushin Il-28 light bombers, which foremost operated by night. The result was an indiscriminate bombing campaign against hundreds of thousands of the Biafrans crammed into mere 4,000 square miles of territory, that caused a major international outrage – in turn raising hopes in Biafra for support from around the world.

Loss of Umuahia and the Liberation of Owerri

It was under these conditions that Colonel Adekunle arrived at the unilateral decision to capture Umuahia. His offensive was initiated in April 1969, with the intention of splitting the remaining Biaffran territory into two by an advance of the 3rd Marine-Commando Division in a northern direction, to link-up with the 2nd Division (which was only 25 miles away from Adekunle's frontlines): his logic was that Biafra would thus also be cut off from its only supply link – the Uli airstrip – and then it would be only a matter of days, weeks at most, until it capitulated.

The operation began well: poorly defended, Umhuahia fell on 22 April, causing the morale of the Biafrans to reach an all-time low. However, their army then counterattacked at Owerri on 29 April, causing a dramatic change: concluding that the 2,000-strong 16th Brigade that garrisoned the place was isolated and had been exposed to constant pressure for months, Adekunle ordered a 'tactical withdrawal.'

Ojukwu and his aides promptly exploited the opportunity: the

Young Biafran soldiers appear to be checking the ammunition for their vz. 58 assault rifles before going into action. The curved magazine of the vz. 58 led many to believe that this Czech weapon was in fact a Soviet Kalashnikov AK-47. Some AK-47s were used by the Biafran Army after being captured during the fighting for Onitsha and Owerri. Other weapons carried by this group include the H&K G-3 carried by the young soldier in the centre of the group. (Author's Collection)

A lonely and forlorn looking soldier is armed with a Lee Enfield rifle and a few rounds of ammunition to defend his trench in the summer of 1969. He is at least protected by a quite substantial bunker built from tree trunks and camouflaged with foliage. Waiting for the advance of a better armed and equipped Nigerian foe must have been frightening, to say the least, for young soldiers like this. (Private Collection)

Biafran Army took over the deserted town and this was quickly converted into their new capital. Not only civil servants began to arrive there, but even some of the local population drifted back to their homes. Eventually, the liberation of Owerri gave Biafra a major morale boost – although the condition of the wider rebellion experienced no major change: actually, by May 1969, the area still under the control of Ojukwu and his followers was reduced to a mere 2,000 square miles.

The War in 1969

The liberation of Owerri was followed by the delivery of new combat aircraft to the Biafrans (see below for details), and a period of particularly bitter fighting on all frontlines. Indeed, the available reports indicate that their armed forces suffered the astounding number of 19,000 wounded alone in April 1969. Unsurprisingly, for the rest of the year, the rebels were limited to operating in rather restrained fashion.

In May 1969, several minor Biafran offensives were launched, including one by the 14th Division in the direction of Port Harcourt – meanwhile protected by a 16,000-strong Nigerian garrison. The same unit also attempted to liberate Elele. Rather unsurprisingly, both efforts remained fruitless.

Around the same time, the 12th Division made repeated attacks on the Nigerian garrison of Aba: however, while putting the defenders under fierce pressure, the Biafran unit simply lacked the resources to seriously threaten its enemy. Similarly, while reaching the outskirts of Okigwi, the 15th Division was unable to achieve a major breakthrough. Overall, the Biafrans had managed to liberate about 1,000 square miles of their territory, but that was about the limit of what they were able to do. Moreover, most of what they held at the time was empty bush, which the Nigerian Army was happy to concede: after all, General Gowon's strategy was to secure urban centres and wear down the Biafran Army in set-piece battles.

With war-weariness spreading on both sides, the frontlines stabilised and the Biafrans and Nigerians both became preoccupied with maintaining the status quo during the following period. This was perhaps most obvious in the Umhuahia area, where both the Nigerian garrison and the Biafran forces surrounding it, de-facto refused to re-open major hostilities. In June 1969 a foreign reporter commented on the state of the Biafran Army and its soldiers:

> Biafran troops are still underdogs. They are ill-fed, ill-clad and still chronically short of ammunition compared with the British and Soviet backed Nigerians. But they appear to have acquired staying power. As one wounded Biafran put it; "Time is on our side. They have the firepower, but we have the stronger will!"[6]

Biafran Guerrilla Campaigns

At the time of the Biafran War, some questioned Ojukwu's decision not to resort to guerrilla warfare. The Biafran attitude in this regard was said to have been influenced by a massacre that took place in Asaba, on the west bank of the Niger River, just inside the Nigerian territory. The place had changed hands several times, but when the Nigerians liberated it after Operation Torch, they came under fire from several remaining Ibo civilians and Biafran soldiers. 'In retaliation', the Nigerians are said to have summarily executed about 700 people, prompting thousands to flee into the bush, where many died of starvation. The Biafran leaders subsequently claimed that the massacre at Asaba would be repeated in any town or village suspected of supporting a guerrilla campaign.

Another reason for not choosing guerrilla warfare was that once the Nigerian Army had passed through a town or village the population returned. In many cases a parallel Biafran administration then took over control of the region under the noses of the Federal Army. If the population of these areas had been seen to be supporting guerrillas then the Nigerians would not have allowed the Ibo population to live in relative peace. Thus, in order to protect the Biafran population it was decided to confine guerrilla attacks to the Mid-West region where the majority of people were non-Ibos.

After August 1968, guerrilla activity in the Mid-West increased substantially and was performed by a mix of insurgents and regular troops. The Biafran Organisation of Freedom Fighters (BOFF) undertook low-intensity operations, while regular units launched infiltration raids. On average there were between 20 and 30 BOFF groups operating in the border region between Nigerian and Biafran territory at any one time: they took full advantage of the unusually long rainy season of 1969 and increased their guerrilla operations. When the Nigerian Army chased the Biafrans out of the Mid-West in September 1967, the non-Ibo population saw them as liberators. However, before long it became obvious that the Federal troops did not distinguish between one group of easterners and another, and treated them all brutally. By late 1968 some of the mistreated eastern minorities were willing to assist their Ibo cousins in striking back at the Nigerian Army. The Mid-West now became the seat of the main guerrilla fighting with BOFF units armed with machetes and a few captured rifles leading the campaign.

Generally, the BOFF groups were loosely organised into the Mid-West Liberation Army (MWLA), which totalled about 3,000 combatants. The MWLA spent most of 1969 making a nuisance of themselves attacking the supply lines of the 2nd Division: small columns of poorly-protected trucks made promising targets. These ambushes netted the MWLA some rifles and other weaponry which allowed them to expand their operations. The activities of the guerrillas were backed up by infiltration raids by battalion size forces of regular Biafran troops. One such raid was described by US correspondent James Wilde in his article 'Attack on a Village,' in which an operation of the 55th Battalion against Umuneke was depicted.

The attacking Biafran troops were mostly barefoot with few uniform items between them and a single bolt action rifle between two or three men. An advance party of the 55th had infiltrated around the back of the village and had set up some of the deadly 'Obunigwe' or – as the men called them – 'Ojukwu's Kettles.' The Biafran plan was to attack the village and force the Nigerians to retreat straight into the path of the Obunigwes. Just before the attack the brigade commander brought a Land Rover full of precious ammunition to be shared out amongst the men. Wilde said that 'The cartridges were counted out like gold nuggets, the .30 calibre machinegun ammunition belts handled like so many rare Grecian urns.'[7]

As Wilde moved up to the trail leading to the village he noted the large groups of unarmed civilians lined up at the sides of the path. The 25-year-old 'brigade commander', Lieutenant-Colonel Lambert Ihenacho explained that these were civilian 'volunteers' who would help take the wounded back to the rear. The attack duly

A machinegun team of the 13th Division wait for the Nigerians in their jungle position with their ZB-53 heavy machinegun in 1969. As if to prove a point all the soldiers are swathed in machinegun belts to show that they have enough ammunition. They are wearing the usual mixture of military and civilian clothing with the gunner wearing a Stetson hat. (Albert Grandolini Collection)

In this action photograph in May 1969 Biafran guerrillas rush though the bush in the Mid-West region to attack an isolated Nigerian platoon. All the men are armed with machetes and hope to capture rifles and other weapons from the enemy. The guerrilla war in the Mid-West was fought by a mixture of civilian fighters like these and regulars operating behind Federal lines. (Author's Collection)

Barefooted but well-armed Biafran troops move through a recently captured village which had been held by Nigerian soldiers. The shortage of boots was a real issue for the Biafrans and any type of footwear would be used when available. Civilian shoes. including fashionable winkle pickers. would be worn and boots were made from any available material including using tires as soles. Apart from cuts which could become infected, a barefoot soldier also had to beware 'jiggers', the larvae of Chigoe Fleas which dug into feet causing horrific sores. (Albert Grandolini Collection)

Two smartly dressed Biafran officers pose proudly with their recently captured H&K G3 assault rifles in the summer of 1969. The officer in the foreground has even adorned himself with a dress uniform 'aiguillette' probably taken from the suitcase of a captured Federal officer. Even in the latter stages of the war resourceful officers could manage to acquire smarter uniforms while their men often dressed in rags. (Author's Collection)

began and soon walking wounded were coming back and handing their precious weapons to other soldiers who then went into the attack. Wilde was surprised to be told that the howitzer firing from the rear was actually a Biafran field gun which loosed off all of its six shells. This short bombardment had been sufficient to cause the Nigerians to withdraw but unfortunately for the Biafrans their main plan failed as they had inconveniently not passed by the waiting Obunigwes. Summing up this operation, Ihennacho said 'We have driven them out of the village. But they have bypassed the mines. Still, we are lucky. Our ammunition lasted until dark, tomorrow they will counterattack and then we will counterattack, and so it will go on.' When asked what he needed to continue the fight he said 'Small arms, ammunition and food. We need more bolt action rifles. They conserve our ammunition.' Asked if Biafra could win the war he replied in typical fashion 'Yes of course. We know what we are fighting for. They don't.'[8]

In May 1969 a two battalion raid by the 6th and 54th battalions was launched across the Niger River. The attack force had a large proportion of ethnic Ibo's from the Mid-West region who were happy to return to their homeland to try and exact revenge on the Nigerians. By June, the guerrilla activity in the Mid-West, including raids by regular Biafran units, had forced the deployment of six Federal battalions. During 1969 both guerrilla and regular army attacks increased and helped to contribute to the Biafran war effort, but in late May the Biafrans suffered a propaganda disaster when ten Italian and one Jordanian oil-workers were killed by MWLA fighters. A further 18 foreign oil-workers were taken hostage and condemned to death by the Biafrans: this group were made up of 14 Italians, 3 Germans and 1 Lebanese who were held until 7 June

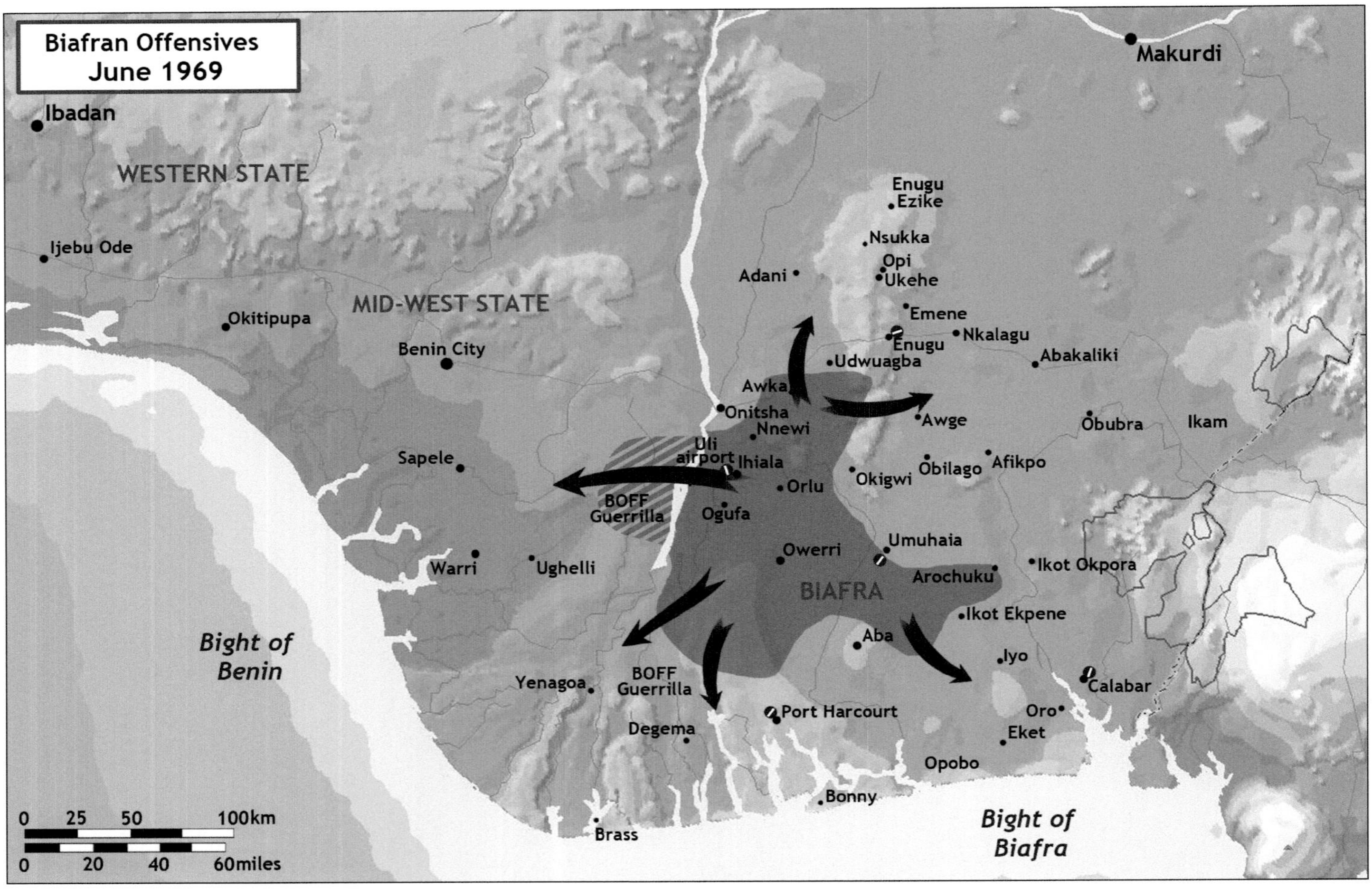

A map showing the (limited) counteroffensives run by the Biafran Army in the first half of 1969, including the liberation of Owerri and the recovery of a few other territories. Also noted is the area within which the BOFF guerrillas were active. (Map by Tom Cooper)

when they were amnestied and freed under world pressure.

The attacks on the oil installations were defended by the Biafrans on the grounds that foreign workers were supporting the Nigerian war economy. Unfortunately for the Biafrans the international press saw it another way and the amount of moral support that they received from abroad was greatly reduced. For once the Biafrans were not seen as the victims but as the aggressors, despite their excuses. As well as the Mid-West there was a low-level guerrilla war

A unit of young Biafran soldiers rest in the jungle before continuing their mission to attack Nigerian supply lines. Much of the fighting by 1969 involved small units of Biafran troops operating as virtual guerrillas in Nigerian controlled territory. By 1969 a large number of Mauser and Lee Enfield rifles were being used by the Biafran Army. The commander of this group of men is carrying a captured Federal Army MG-3, the modernised version of the Second World War MG-42 machinegun. (Private Collection)

A lone Biafran sentry stands guard outside buildings recently captured from the Nigerians at Okwala Junction in June 1969. Although his painted camouflage uniform carries no visible ranks he is probably at least an NCO because he is armed with a Czech vz. 58 assault rifle. Another clue to his rank is the pen sticking out of his breast pocket, an item usually reserved for officers in the Biafran Army. (Author's Collection)

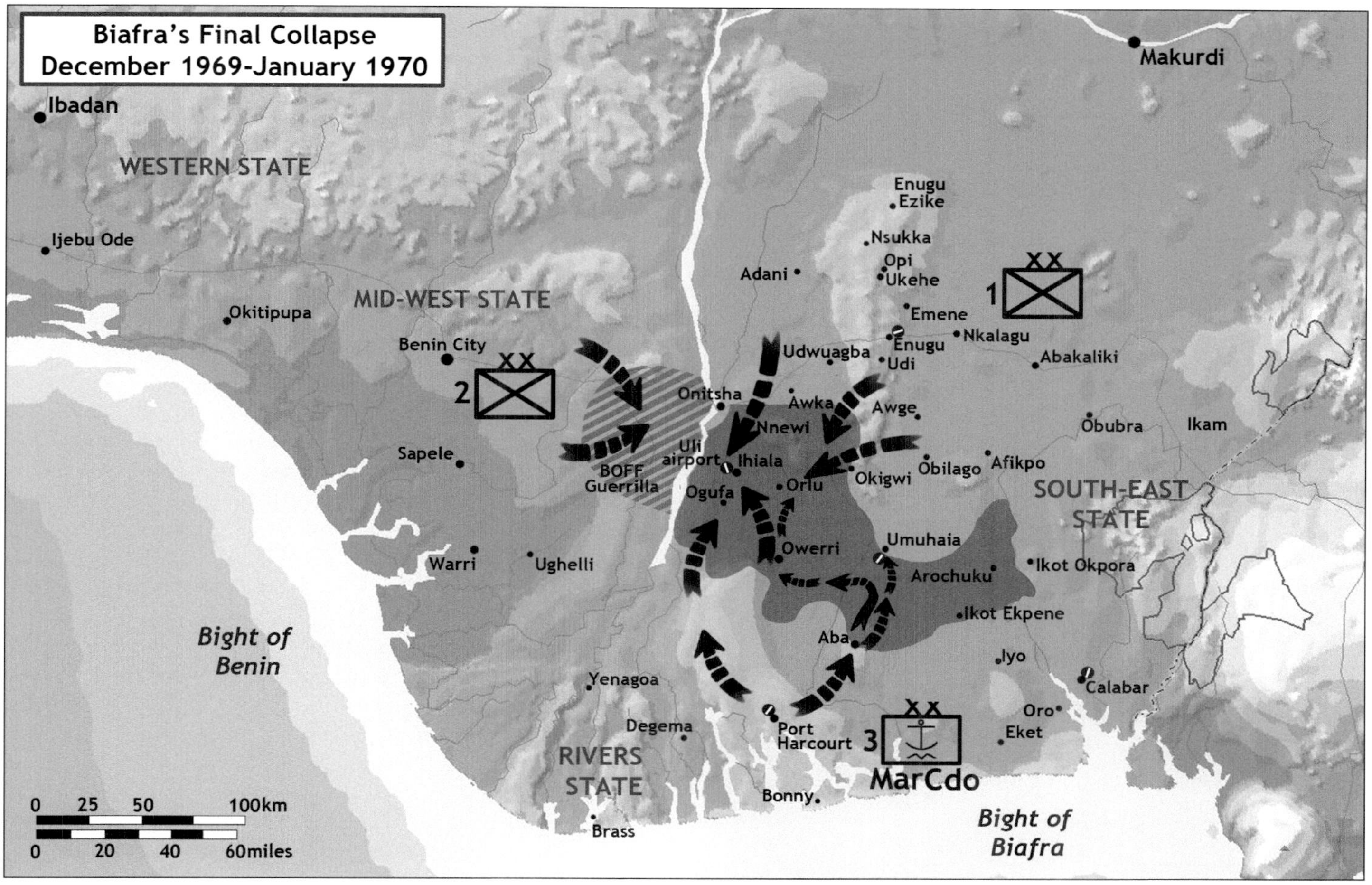

A map showing the Nigerian offensives of late 1969 and early 1970 – the final phase of the war: notable are offensives by the 1st Division in the north and the 3rd Marine-Commando Division in the south, which split the remaining Biafran territory into two. (Map by Tom Cooper)

in the south of occupied Biafra in 1969. These attacks by Biafran guerrillas were led by Rangers who had been specially trained from 1967 for this purpose (see above). Although not on the same scale as the fighting in the Mid-West, the southern campaign did threaten the Nigerian Army. Amongst others, they repeatedly interrupted the supply lines of the 3rd Marine-Commando Division and the 1st Division. Still, and even though the guerrilla activity continued until the end of the war, it was still seen by the Nigerian Army as just a nuisance: the reason was that it never severely affected its war effort.

Decline and Fall of the Biafran Army, 1969-1970

Even though the Biafrans had seen a number of military successes in the first nine months of 1969, these only served to mask the growing crisis in the country. These local victories had been great for the morale of the civilian population who listened to the Biafran radio broadcasts. At the frontline however, the day-to-day slog and suffering of the ordinary soldier caused a renewed – and then a steep – decline in morale. Many Biafran soldiers had been on the verge of starvation throughout the war and had got used to having empty stomachs. But, after two years of bitter war, everybody was at breaking point, and only sheer determination kept them fighting.

In March 1969, a journalist interviewed two Biafran soldiers and asked when they had last eaten; 'Barely once today, perhaps again tomorrow, who knows?'[9]

The Biafran determination to continue fighting was demonstrated when he asked why they continued to fight: 'We must, we simply must.'[10]

By September the troops were officially getting one meal a day and got little if any pay with deductions for non-existent food from their wages. They also complained about the lack of uniforms and medical care to visiting journalists. And still, somehow the Biafran Army fought on while its men slowly starved to death on their feet, and with sentries fainting at their posts. Most were weakened to the point where it took several men to lift weapons and ammunition that one man could have carried if he had been fed adequately. Digging trenches and any other manual work became more difficult and most soldiers were operating on 'autopilot'. Soldiers also began suffering from a condition they called 'Gowon's Boots' which was the swelling of the feet due to Kwashiorkor.[11] Other starving soldiers looked like living skeletons underneath their uniforms due the affliction known as Marasmus. By October there were increasing reports of sagging morale in many Biafran units – all for the lack of food.

The food supply available to the government had been severely affected when starving civilians had harvested thousands of acres of cassava growing to the south of Owerri. Other food-growing areas fell with the loss of the large garra-growing region (garra is an edible root) near Aba, again severely affecting the acute food shortage. Reportedly, the army was subsequently getting about 10 percent of all available food from distribution centres, which meant that soldiers only had about one meal every four days.

This paltry supply of food usually ended up at brigade level where some officers chose to share some with their families before sending the remains to their men. Even though the lion's share was often kept at the various headquarters, rear echelon staff were said by late 1969 to be getting a meal every other day. There were many examples of abuse of food supplies by some officers, with one

Brigadier-General Philip Effiong seen here in 1969 inspecting a captured Federal grenade played an important part in ending the war. When Ojukwu left Biafra for exile Effiong was given responsibility for organising the Biafran Armed Forces surrender in January 1970. He was treated by some Nigerian officers as a long lost friend when he attended the surrender ceremony at Dodan Barracks Lagos. (Author's Collection)

unnamed brigade commander taking it to extremes. His unit had received 4 goats to give to his men a treat at Christmas in 1969 but he insisted on taking two and a half of their carcasses for himself and his entourage. Another unscrupulous officer got his unit's food ration and before the troops could see it, he took 50% for his own and his family's needs. Of course, there were some officers who didn't abuse their positions but in reality it took a strong man to deny his own family food. How the ordinary soldier survived the last months of the war is hard to say, although they resorted to more and more desperate measures. Some officers ordered the hijacking of relief trucks taking food to civilian feeding stations in order to feed their men. Colonel Ojukwu was unlikely to stop this behaviour and he emphasised that the soldiers should be given priority. When some Biafran civilian volunteers complained about the commandeering of relief supplies in September he gave them short shrift. He is quoted as saying, 'A young able-bodied school teacher who prefers to distribute relief when he should be fighting his country's war is not only unpatriotic, but is doing a woman's work.'[12] As far as he was concerned the army and its men came first because if they were unable to fight the civilians would be slaughtered by the Federal Army anyway. As in other cases of mass famine throughout history, eventually starvation led desperate people to even greater crimes. Cases of cannibalism began to emerge during 1969, with some well organised gangs ambushing victims. Colonel Ojukwu ordered the execution in late 1969 of 8 civilians and 2 army officers who were involved in the 'trade'. According to reports they attacked lone and straggling soldiers who were sold 'alive' to customers for £50. A dead victim was sold at a bargain price of £5, presumably because it was harder to keep them fresh in the heat.

Operation Tailwind

On 17 November 1968, the Nigerian Chief-of-Staff, Brigadier-General Hassan Usman Katsina ordered the launching of an offensive to 'liberate what was left of the rebel held areas.' The Nigerians had been building up stocks of ammunition and bringing in fresh troops to make sure that the Biafrans were defeated before the start of the rainy season in April 1970. Facing this onslaught was a Biafran Army which had basically had enough, and the number of desertions had reached alarming proportions. By December 1969 many Biafran troops were receiving one small meal a day – if they were lucky: actually, most were getting one meal every three days, and some only once a week. When they did receive food, it was usually in the form of dry 'garri' to which they added water to form a kind of porridge and was then 'smoked.' This food however had virtually no nutritional value and had no vitamins or protein in it.

Exhausted Biafran soldiers rest in a jungle clearing in the last few months of the war when many soldiers were literally starving. The Biafrans had managed to continue their resistance during 1969 but the constant hunger they faced sapped even the most resolute in their ranks. Even as the majority of the army was laying down their weapons in January 1970 a few units continued to resist for a few more days. (Author's Collection)

A member of General Effiong's bodyguard who has escorted him to the surrender meeting with Federal officers in January 1970 hugs a Nigerian soldier. For many soldiers on both sides the sudden end of the war was a relief and former pre-1967 comrades were often genuinely pleased to meet again. The Nigerian soldier is armed with the latest Soviet AKM assault rifle while the Biafran soldier has handed in his vz. 58 to the Federal officials. (Peter Obe)

Unsurprisingly, when the main thrust of the 12th and 17th Brigades of the Nigerian Army pushed through the middle of the Biafran territory on 22 December, the Biafrans began to collapse. By 25 December, the Federals had reached the northern border of the Biafran-controlled territory a few miles outside Umhuahia, while two divisions – the 12th and the 15th – were virtually destroyed. What was left of Biafra by the end of 1969 were two isolated enclaves with most of their defenders waiting for the final blows to be struck.

January 1970

By the dawn of 1970 the Biafran Army was in its final death throes with only isolated units continuing to resist the Nigerian advances: what was left of the once proud armed forces was at breaking point, with their morale finally broken by the years of fruitless struggle and starvation. Still, even then, Ojukwu was hoping his troops could hold out for a while longer, causing the Nigerians to lose heart. Counting on the lack of unity in the Federal camp, he was convinced that the commanders of the disparate units of the Nigerian Army would fall out with each other.

On 7 January 1970, the Nigerians re-launched their offensive by attacking the Biafrans at several sectors simultaneously. The 13th and 18th Brigades advanced in the east, while the 14th, 15th, 16th and 19th Brigades moved into the larger western enclave, which included Owerri and the Uli airstrip. The Biafran 15th Division had been destroyed in the west and the sad remnants of the 12th Division melted away, leaving the 11th Division and the 4th Commando Division as the only viable forces.

Ojukwu's standpoint about continuing the war changed only a day later, when Major-General Madiebo telephoned General Effiong to tell him his men could no longer resist the Nigerians. At a meeting arranged for 9 January 1970, Ojukwu spoke of his hope of holding the enemy out of Owerri, even though knowing that the town was already largely under Federal control. Still, nobody challenged his standpoint. Indeed, Ojukwu claimed that Colonel Achuzia was poised to lead 2,000 troops into a major offensive in Owerri, even though Achuzia was at the meeting and knew that the only troops remaining were his own bodyguards. Still, nobody challenged the leader's standpoint: even Achuzia remained silent. Ojukwu then brought in a number of civilian leaders and gave them the same lecture but again was unable to convince them. Finally realising the war was over, the Biafran leader then gathered his family and entourage (a forlorn group of three aides), packed them into a Mercedes-Benz staff car, together with three tonnes of luggage, and drove to the Uli airstrip. From there, they were flown out to Gabon, where Ojukwu promised he would 'never surrender but continue fighting on in the bush.' As with so many of his other statements, these proved to be hollow words.

Meanwhile, the command of the Biafran Army was handed over to its last Chief-of-Staff, General Philip Effiong. He immediately looked around for a way to end the hopeless war. By the next day – 10 January 1970 – the last remaining small towns still in Biafran hands, Utoru, Arochuka, and Ohafia, fell to the advancing Nigerians, as the rebel armed forces melted away. Frederick Forsyth wrote about these days; 'A unit on the Southern Front, exhausted beyond caring and out of ammunition, quietly stripped off its uniforms and faded into the bush.'[13]

On 12 January 1970, Effiong unilaterally brought the curtain down on the rebellion, announcing the capitulation of all the Biafran forces. A – surprisingly friendly – surrender ceremony attended by him and the last handful of Biafran officers took place at Dodan Barracks, in Lagos, three days later. Old, pre-civil war officer-comrades embraced each other like the old friends they were and pointed the way to a hoped-for reconciliation. For the ordinary Biafran soldier however, the future did not look bright: there were too many bad feelings, and these were to be felt – severely – for years longer. Although no large-scale massacres of the Biafran soldiers and civilians took place, life was hard for the survivors for most of the 1970s. Even to this day, the surviving Biafran veterans campaign to receive a pension for their service in 1967-1970.

Chapter 6
Biafra's Naval and Air War

Naval warfare in the Nigerian Civil War began with one of those rumours which were prevalent in the already divided country in the weeks before the outbreak of war. There was great jubilation in the east when reports were received about the sinking of the Nigerian Navy's flagship NNS *Nigeria*. The *Nigeria* was a frigate and was by far the largest and most powerful ship in the Nigerian Navy. It was seen by the Biafrans as one of the greatest threats to their survival at the start of the war. In the weeks before the official secession of Biafra, the *Nigeria* was supposed to have been sunk in Lagos Harbour by eastern guerrillas. Although the reports were certainly exaggerated it was the case that some of the ship's crewmen from the east did manage to sabotage some of the Nigerian Navy's ships. Reports said that seaman of eastern origin were leaving their posts and quietly returning home throughout the last weeks of April. On 24 April, a full month before the secession of the east, 30 crewmen were reported to have deserted but not before sabotaging their ships. Before leaving, the crewmen had damaged some of the electronic equipment in several of the ships. The NNS *Nigeria* was particularly targeted by the saboteurs, with eastern technicians damaging or stealing vital navigational equipment. According to the Nigerians however, with the help of their foreign suppliers all the damaged and stolen gear was replaced by the time the war began. The naval war between the Nigerian Navy and the newly raised Biafran Navy was now to prove to be yet another 'David versus Goliath' affair.

The Biafran Navy was formed at the time of secession to try and protect the coastal and inland ports which were so vital to the survival of Biafra. It was made up of a handful of smaller conventional naval vessels, homemade gunboats and monitors, and confiscated speed boats. Biafra's Navy had a number of 'acquired' merchant ships that were converted into combat ships. Its only combat ship was the BNS *Vigilance* which was an ex-Royal Navy Ford class seaward defence vessel which had been sold to the Nigerian Navy. During its Royal Navy service, it was called HMS *Montford* and renamed NNS *Ibadan* in Nigerian service. *Ibadan* was renamed BNS *Vigilance* when it was captured by the Biafrans and was found to be armed with a single Bofors 40mm anti-aircraft gun. Unfortunately for the Biafrans, the Bofors was faulty and jammed after firing 2 or 3 shells. The *Vigilance* had a rather short career in Biafran service surviving from late May until September 1967. Beside the single Navy vessel, the Biafrans relied on merchant ships converted into a naval role. The Biafrans had a Nigerian Port Authority Thornycroft tugboat which was armed with a 105mm howitzer and renamed BNS *Ikwerre*. A Nigerian Port Authority cutter was given the designation PC101 and was well armed with a 6-pounder anti-tank gun and a Bofors 40mm anti-aircraft gun. The PC101 had a short career, being sunk in July 1968 along with the PC202; an ex-Nigerian tugboat which had been armed with 105mm howitzer. Another tugboat, the PC203, with unknown armament was also sunk in the heavy fighting of September 1968. This only left the PC204, a medium sized merchant ship which was pushed into action in 1969 and may have survived the war. The Biafran Navy also employed a real mixture of ex-Shell Oil vessels in the early stages of the war. In their former roles these vessels had been used to supply the oil facilities and to ferry staff between locations. These vessels included two oil supply craft with shallow draughts which were converted into troop carriers. Renamed the *Nsiko* and *Pepeye*, the two boats had very loud engines and sounded like large car engines without the mufflers, and thus they could not be used in any covert operations. A few ex-Shell Oil Holland Launches, or H/Ls, which had been used to transport personnel to various sites were also converted into troop carriers. They were armed with 6-pounder anti-tank guns which were placed at the front of the launches. Shell Oil barges were also converted into mobile artillery platforms with sandbagged emplacements installed on their decks and were armed with 105mm howitzers. These were then towed into position by other vessels to lay down fire in support of the navy. Some vessels were found to totally unsuitable when used outside the roles that they had been designed for. The reality was that the Biafrans had to use whatever ships were available and find ways to utilise them for their war

Small motorboats like these were used to patrol the small rivers and creeks in the south of the country. Right until the end of the war the Biafrans tried to contest control of the Niger Delta region. Sometimes small boats like this were mounted with light machineguns although often the only armament they had was the rifles and sub-machineguns of their crews. (Private Collection)

effort. Biafra also tried to buy naval vessels on the world market, but no one who was legitimate was willing to sell them warships. There were also reports that the Biafrans approached the USA to obtain examples of their fibreglass PTI boats that were being used in large numbers in Vietnam. Of course, their pleas fell on deaf ears as the Americans did not want to become involved in the conflict.

Apart from the seagoing ships of the Navy there were an undocumented number of wooden fishing boats converted into improvised gunboats. Before secession Biafran officials had requested several shipyards to build wooden fishing vessels. The hulls of the boats were protected with metal plates which had firing ports cut into them. A crude metal plate superstructure was fitted to provide protection for the crew and their roofs were made from corrugated sheeting. They were fitted with Volkswagen car engines and armed with 1 or 2 machineguns and were used to patrol the inland waterways of the south and west of the country. These improvised warships were capable of taking on Nigerian protected merchant ships but usually came off worse against Nigerian Navy vessels. The Biafrans were looking to utilise any boat or ship that they got their hands on to turn into a warship. One scheme involved a plan to arm a civilian dredging vessel with hidden troops and concealed guns. The idea was that the dredger and its 12 crew and another 12 soldiers would sail into the sea around the port of Bonny. They would then wait for a Nigerian Navy ship to come along and act suspiciously. In normal circumstances a Nigerian patrol boat would hail any ship which they could not identify and tell the crew they were going to board. When they pulled alongside the dredger the hidden soldiers would fire at the Nigerian crew, take over their ship and bring it back to join the ranks of their navy. The Biafran Navy commander claimed he got the idea from a scene in the 1964 war film *Guns of Navarone*. However, on the one occasion that the dredger went to sea they waited in vain as no Nigerian vessels came anywhere near them. Conditions were too choppy and the dredger was not really built for rough seas and so it was not used in this role again.

It must have been difficult to find crews for the Biafran Navy, bearing in mind the fact that their ships were totally outgunned. The Navy's personnel came from two sources; with a handful of ex-Nigerian Navy crews being joined by civilian volunteers. Most of the crewmen were recruited from the offshore oil industry with a majority being ex-Shell Oil employees. There were enough oil supply crewmen and marine engineers to keep the ships and boats of the Navy working.

Gunboats of the Biafran Navy are seen gathered together at one of the river ports from where they operated against the far more powerful Federal Navy. Tug boats and other commercial vessels were turned into warships with the addition of machineguns and lashed down artillery pieces. Many crewmen had brought their boats into Biafran service from their former employers in the oil industry. (Via Albert Grandolini)

There are few photographs available of the ships of the Biafran Navy and this poor quality image shows the PC202. This ex-Nigerian tugboat was reported to be armed with a 105mm howitzer whose covered barrel is visible in the background. The PC202 is seen back in port having been involved with a battle with Nigerian ships in 1968. According to reports the PC202 was sunk in July 1968 along with its sister ship the PC101. (Private Collection)

The Navy at War

The reality for the Biafran Navy throughout the war was that its vessels could only really act as a nuisance to the far more powerful Federal Navy. Its main role was to try and fight any Nigerian ships that ventured up the rivers and tributaries of the Delta region along the Atlantic coast. Rarely did the Biafran Navy venture away from the shelter of the river system to take on the Nigerians in open sea. As with nearly every other aspect of the Nigerian Civil War the naval battles were pretty one-sided affairs. Despite a number of defeats, the Biafrans were somehow able to keep fighting and had some vessels afloat until the last months of the war. At the start of the war the Nigerian Navy sent most of its ships from their bases in the west of the country to impose a naval blockade on the east. Once the Nigerian ships, led by NNS *Nigeria*, had arrived off the coast of Biafra any larger ships could not bring in supplies. Although a few small boats might be able to slip past the blockade larger vessels were usually intercepted by the Navy. With the blockade in place the Nigerian Navy's role was now widened to assisting the army. Their ships were to co-operate with the newly raised 3rd Division to capture the major ports on the Atlantic coast. In addition, the Navy sent its smaller vessels up the river system to capture Biafra's river ports in order to stop the Biafran Navy from using them. Although the Biafrans feared NNS *Nigeria* at sea, it was far too large to sail up the rivers of Biafra and it was left to the Nigerian Navy's smaller vessels to challenge the Biafrans along the river system. Besides the main ports, like Calabar in the east and Degema in the west, there

A platoon of troops is seen crossing one of the many rivers and streams of Biafra in a flat bottomed boat. The river network in Biafra caused issues for both armies especially when many bridges had been blown by the retreating Biafrans. Neither side had enough boats nor was any civilian craft that the Federals and Biafrans could get hold of confiscated. (Private Collection)

The famous Polish adventurer pilot Jean Zumba stands in front of the B-26R he flew for a number of weeks in the summer of 1967. In his auto-biography he described how the ex-US attack bomber had to be adapted so that it could perform a bomber role. After flying a number of missions, he was reported to have left Biafra having found the strain of constant action too much. (Albert Grandolini Collection)

were other ports situated in the Niger Delta. While it was up to NNS *Nigeria* to intercept larger merchant ships, the smaller ships of the Nigerian Navy would battle the Biafran ships. Smaller vessels like NNS *Ogoja* and NNS *Sapele* were to be the main opponents for the makeshift Biafran Navy. The *Ogoja* was to be a particular thorn in the Biafran side with its 76mm main armament, a Bofors 40mm and five 20mm Oerlikons. After several years of service during the war, the ex-US Navy patrol craft was to be lost at sea under unknown circumstances in October 1969.

Bonny Island, off the coast of south Biafra, fell to the Nigerians in late July 1967 in an historic first amphibious landing by a Third World navy and land forces. The island was held by a single Nigerian battalion as the rest of the army was preoccupied with the Biafrans' mid-west invasion in August. For the next few months attempts were made by the Biafran Army and Navy with their gunboats to take back the strategically vital island. During the battles along the coast in September, the Biafran Navy's converted gunboats did manage to sink the Nigerian Navy gunboat NNS *Sapele*, as well as a few transport boats. The loss of the *Sapele*, along with all her crew including its young commander Lieutenant Sereki, was a heavy blow for the Nigerians. Despite the brave efforts of the Biafran gunboats, the Nigerians held on to Bonny whose garrison was soon reinforced by troops freed by the defeat of the Mid-West invasion. Nigerian naval and land forces now concentrated on the Niger Delta river ports with the Navy landing 3rd Division forces in September. Using small boats, the Nigerian troops were able to take the ports of Warri, Sapele and Koko during the month. They were faced by small units of Biafran troops and a few motorboats during their advance. Once the small ports had been secured, the Nigerians began planning for a much larger operation to take the major port of Calabar in the south-east. The port was held by the Biafran 9th Battalion with support from the only available Biafran Navy gunboat. As at Bonny Island, the Nigerians were able to launch a well organised amphibious landing at Calabar using barges and landing ships to put troops of the 3rd Division ashore. The several thousand Nigerians were soon able to brush aside the few hundred Biafrans and take the port. When Nigerian troops landed at Calabar on 19 October they cut off Biafra from access to neighbouring Cameroon by sea. As the land border with Cameroon had already been blocked by Nigerian troops Biafra was now surrounded on all sides. When the port fell the Biafrans suffered another blow when the Nigerian Navy captured the gunrunning Dutch merchant ship *Jazine*. The ship's cargo contained 11,000 double barrelled shotguns which had been earmarked for the Biafran militia. It also had 257 cases of shotgun shells and 389 reels of newsreel destined for the Biafran propaganda agency.

Although the Biafrans still controlled the inland port and city of Port Harcourt until mid-1968, its excellent port facilities were of little use as long as the naval blockade remained in place. Port Harcourt was to prove more difficult to conquer than the other ports and it was to take almost a year for the Nigerians to capture it. Along the coast and in the delta region the Biafran and Nigerian Navies continued to fight small naval engagements during late 1967 and early 1968. In May 1968 a rather bizarre sea battle was fought between improvised Biafran gunboats and a Nigerian armed trawler. The trawler was, strangely, armed with a Panhard AML armoured car which had been strapped to its deck. Regardless of the bizarre weaponry of the Nigerian vessel it managed to sink both Biafran boats using the car's 60mm mortar. The defence of Port Harcourt in May also involved PC101 which was armed with a 6-pounder anti-tank gun and a Bofors anti-aircraft gun. In addition, the PC202, a converted tugboat which was armed with a 105mm howitzer lashed to its deck, also took part. During a first sea battle with Nigerian ships the two 'gunboats' managed to sink several of the enemy boats. Despite these Nigerian losses Port Harcourt fell on 19 May costing the Biafrans not only the major port facilities but also the airport. The 3rd Marine Division were again the victors in the battle for Port Harcourt and a month later they took Biafra's last port of Degema. This south-western town fell on 19 June and from then on the Biafran Navy was going to have to operate from smaller river ports. By the end of July the remaining gunboats, PC101 and 202, had been badly damaged and put out of action.

The headquarters of the Biafran Navy was now established at the lakeside town of Oguta, on Lake Oguta, to the north-west of Port Harcourt. Oguta came under pressure in the summer of 1968 and fell to a river-borne attack of the Nigerian Army on 9 September. Because Oguta was dangerously close to Uli airfield the Biafrans had to recapture it at all costs. All the Biafrans' available resources were pushed into the liberation of Oguta which took place on 13 September. The town was once again the HQ of the Navy which in reality hardly existed at all apart from wooden river boats. With no larger vessels available the Navy now consisted of a number of river boats usually armed with machineguns and the odd mortar.

There were a number of tributaries which flowed southwards from Lake Oguta to the sea including the Orashi River. For the next year a low-level campaign continued with river-borne raids launched by the Biafrans and Nigerians on enemy positions. Navy personnel often found themselves seconded to army units and small units of naval crew fought as soldiers for the rest of the war. In September 1969 a little reported campaign took place along this river which was overseen by the Biafran Navy commander, Captain W. A. Anuku. He had been the commander of NNS *Nigeria* before the war and was now in command of a few wooden river boats. His personal bravery and that of his boat crews resulted in several awards which were never presented, however, as there were no medals available.

Riverine Warfare

Once the ports of Biafra had been captured the waterborne campaigns of the civil war took place along the inland waterways. In an attempt to disrupt the river traffic on the Niger River and its tributaries a powerboat attack force was created in early 1968. A few Chris-Craft luxury powerboats were confiscated from the Port Harcourt Sailing Club. They were lightly armed with a single vz. 59 machinegun mounted at the front. Nigerian supply boats and small freighters with small military escorts were using the rivers in Federal occupied south-west Biafra to move supplies to their units. Although the Biafran Navy had a commanding officer, Commander Winifred Anuku, this new venture was a covert operation. It was under the command of a freebooting Italian mercenary, Giorgio Norbiatto, who laid in wait for single Nigerian vessels to pass. Two successful attacks were made on isolated ships with the first operation netting a large quantity of weapons and equipment. It was claimed that the booty from the first attack included five Land Rovers and an amount of 7.62mm ammunition said to be in the millions of rounds. The list of captured gear included thousands of camouflage uniforms en-route to the Federal Army, which was short of replacement uniforms. A second attack saw 10 tons of 'Soviet' mortar bombs being captured, although these were probably for the British types that the Nigerian had. A large number of hand grenades were also taken from the second ship and two defensive 20mm Oerlikon anti-aircraft guns were dismounted from it. Shortly after the end of the second attack, Norbiatto was killed in a skirmish, and there

This poor-quality photograph purports to show one of the two B-25 Mitchell bombers which flew for Biafra in 1967. In the image it appears that four nose guns have been added to the bomber at some point possibly in its previous service. Some wild rumours in Biafra in the summer of 1967 claimed that the B-25s and B-26s that were in service were in fact a squadron of jet bombers! (Leif Hellstrom via Mike Draper)

A Biafran ground crewman pulls the camouflage from the fuselage of the Air Force's RB-26P before it goes on a bombing mission. This aircraft had previously flown in a civilian role as an aerial survey aircraft and had of course been converted back into a military role. (Albert Grandolini Collection)

were no more operations launched on the same scale. Even smaller vessels were also used by the Biafrans and these were usually small private motorboats which could carry a handful of troops.

Biafra's Air Power

When the civil war began neither side had a modern combat air force. The Nigerians were in the early stages of developing their air arm and did have West German Dornier Do-27 and Italian Piaggio P.149D trainers as well as a few DC-3 transports. If the civil war had not occurred, then the Nigerians would have formed a combat force in due course. Upon the outbreak of the civil war, Nigeria immediately began searching for modern fighter-bombers and bombers to improve the potency of their Air Force. Nigerian officials asked the UK and other NATO countries to sell them suitable aircraft but were turned down. They then approached the Soviet Bloc and agreements were reached for a number of Czech L-29 jet trainers and Soviet MiG-17 fighter-bombers. When the first of these jet aircraft arrived in Nigeria in mid-August the Biafrans knew that the handful of old aircraft they had would soon be totally dominated. The Biafrans had slightly stolen the march on the Nigerians by acquiring their first combat aircraft. They would have to do more if they were to win the air war.

Even before the secession of Biafra in May 1967 was formally announced, the easterners were trying to acquire aircraft for their projected air force. On 23 April 1967, eastern troops hijacked a Nigerian Airways Fokker Friendship F-27 which was on a flight from Benin City to Lagos. The plane was flown by its crew to the eastern state capital at Enugu and its 27 passengers were released and sent back to Benin City in Mid-West Nigeria by road. The Biafrans also obtained two DC-3 transport aircraft which may have been converted into bombers before the fighting began. One was stolen from Nigeria Airways in early April 1967 while a Ghana Airways plane was impounded in the east in May. In the immediate aftermath of the secession on 30 May, the now Biafrans tried to buy combat aircraft, especially bombers. Biafra's arms agents scoured the surplus aircraft market and managed to find some vintage aircraft which, although not ideal, could be used as bombers. It took until 29 June for the first 'combat' aircraft to arrive in the breakaway state. This was a civilianised Douglas B-26R Invader ground attack bomber which was delivered by a Cuban air crew who promptly disappeared out of the country. A second B-26 Invader, which was the RB-26P version, arrived at Enugu having been bought from a French aerial survey company. Two Second World War era B-25 Mitchell medium bombers were also purchased from a Miami based arms dealer. Both of these aircraft were based at Port Harcourt and were flown on a number of bombing raids by Friedrich Herz and several other pilots.

Flying Adventurers

To fly the hodgepodge of old bombers and converted cargo planes they had acquired from various sources Biafra relied on a group of exotic foreign pilots. The most famous of these pilots was Jean, or Jan, Zumbach (also known as John Brown) a Swiss-born Polish veteran of the Second World War. Joining the Polish Army in 1934 he had transferred to the Air Force and was a fighter pilot in 1939 but was injured with a broken leg when the Germans invaded in 1939. During the Second World War he served in the Royal Air Force, taking part in the Battle of Britain. He served in various roles in the air and in training colleges during the rest of the war before being demobbed in 1946. In 1962 he appeared in Katanga, the breakaway region of Congo, and was given the job of organising its tiny air force. Having got a taste for mercenary flying, he turned up in Biafra in July 1967 offering his services to the desperate secessionists. He flew the B-26R for about a month, carrying out a number of bombing raids before he began to show the strain of constant combat. Zumbach left Biafra in August and he was replaced by a rather mysterious Frenchman called Monsiour Durang who flew the bomber for a few weeks until it was put out of action in early September 1967. Another pilot who was literally larger than life was Barry 'Howg' McWhurter, aged 42 and weighing 300lbs. He was reported to have flown the B-26R for a short period before the other foreign pilots arrived but there is little information on his flying record. The B-25 Mitchell bombers were flown by a confusing mix of foreign pilots during their few weeks of service. One was a 40-year-old West German pilot called Friedrich Herz who had flown for the Luftwaffe in the Second World War. Herz flew one of the B-25s for a few weeks but the constant strain of keeping the aged planes in the air began to tell on him. He was joined by a Portuguese pilot, Gil Pinto de Sousa, who had flown on missions over Portuguese West Africa (Angola) in the early 1960s. He arrived in Biafra via the island of Sao Tome in early September 1967 and after an interview with the Air Force commander Lieutenant-Colonel Chude Sokei he signed a contract. In his book *Shadows* Michael Draper says that the B-25s were also flown by a Cuban pilot who called himself 'Captain Yas' and an unknown US pilot.

Biafra's Helicopters

As the Biafrans looked around desperately for any aircraft that could be used against the Nigerians, at the start of the war they confiscated a number of helicopters that belonged to foreign oil companies and were taken over by the Biafrans at Port Harcourt. The helicopters were three British Westland Widgeons and a single French Alouette II. They were re-painted in camouflage patterns and re-badged with the new Biafran roundel. During the first weeks of the fighting the Alouette, in particular, was used on primitive bombing raids over Nigerian lines. These bombing raids consisted of the co-pilot throwing grenades and homemade bombs out of the door of the helicopter. The other helicopters could not be flown on bombing missions purely due to the shortage of pilots. There were three Biafran pilots, Augustus Okpe, Godwin Chukwu and Willy Murray-Bruce available to fly the helicopters, but they were overworked. They received training on the various helicopters from a French instructor and began to fly them on improvised bombing raids. Godwin Chukwu flew one of the helicopters in support of the Biafran Navy in early August. One Widgeon was eventually flown on a mission in early 1968 but it had to be crash landed by the crew and they were set upon by Biafran civilians who refused to believe that the pilots were not saboteurs, and unfortunately the two men were lynched.

Half a dozen mixed Alouette II and III helicopters were acquired via a Luxembourg trading company and several Biafran pilots were reported to have been trained to fly them by a French instructor. They were used to transport high ranking officers in the first months of the war but their role became too risky when the Nigerian MiG-17s began to dominate the skies over Biafra. In total the Biafrans had managed in addition to acquire during 1967, 4 Alouette II light helicopters, 2 Alouette III medium helicopters, 3 Westland Widgeons and 2 Hiller UH-12Es. Due to the lack of helicopter pilots most of them were to be captured during the Nigerian advances in 1968.

The 27-year-old Swedish pilot Gunnar Haglund gives the thumbs up before going on a ground attack mission. Flying MFI-9B was fairly easy for the experienced Swedish pilots who arrived to fly with Count Von Rosen in 1969. It was the size and slow speed of the MFI-9B which was its best defence against both anti-aircraft and air to air attack by the Nigerians MiG-17s. Painted light blue underneath the small planes were hard to pick out in the sky likewise the fast jet fighter bombers found it hard to find them when flying above because of the green paint they were camouflaged with. (Author's Collection)

Biafran Air Crews in 1967

A number of Biafran air crew and ground crew had escaped from their Nigerian squadrons before the secession. They were in various stages of their training and there were no pilots trained to fly larger aircraft like the B-25 and B-26 bombers. Instead they filled the other air crew roles including observer, air gunner and co-pilot alongside the mercenary pilots. Two Biafrans eventually flew the bombers and when the second air force was formed in early 1969, a number of Biafran pilots flew the MFI-9Bs beside the Swedish pilots (see below). Amongst the air crew of the B-26s and B-25s were Godwin Ezeilo, and Tony Alaribe who acted as an air gunner. Biafrans were also given the task of producing bombs for the B-26s and B-25s with a man called Willy Achukwe in charge. Achukwe used his knowledge from his previous profession as a fireworks maker to produce the bombs. He and his mechanics worked at the railway repair shop at Enugu train station and made bombs out of shell casings filled with nails, broken bottles and kerosene. Other bombs were made from oil drums and gas cylinders which were also filled with scrap metal and other sharp objects.

Early Bombing Raids

The Biafrans' first Second World War vintage American B-26 Invader was readied to go into action and was fitted out by ex-Nigerian Air Force armourers. They armed it with heavy machineguns and rockets in time for it to be taken on its first combat mission a few days later. On 9 July, the B-26 flew three missions in the north and bombed Nigerian positions at Nsukka. The aircraft caught a column of Nigerian troops moving southwards and dropped at least one bomb on them. When asked how the raid had gone, the pilot replied; "Frankly I don't know, but we made a lot of smoke." Another raid hit three targets, Kano, Kaduna and Makurdi Air Base without causing too much damage. The Federal DC-3 transport planes, fortunately for the Nigerians, were in Lagos picking up 105mm shells and mortar rounds. The next raid on the 26th saw a B-26, and a DC-3 transport converted into a bomber, attacking NNS *Nigeria* anchored off the Biafran coast as part of its blockade duties. On 10 August one of the B-26s bombed the Federal air base at Kaduna and caused a lot of damage to its buildings and hangars. Amongst the casualties on the ground was a West German technician who was killed, while two of his colleagues were injured. They had been maintaining the Federal Air Force's Dornier DO-27 trainers with which they had trained Nigerian pilots. Two days later two B-26s attacked the town of Lokoja and succeeded in destroying the Federal Army barracks there. They were also reported to have badly damaged a ferry taking Nigerian troops across the river close to the town. At this early stage in the war one thing that the mercenary pilots did not have to worry about was anti-aircraft guns as the Federal Army did not yet have any. On 16 August a single B-26 supported the invasion of the Mid-West by bombing a Nigerian force moving into the region to fight the Biafran 101st Division. In a two-day bombing mission beginning on the 19th, a single B-26 attacked Kano Airport damaging a number of buildings. It also destroyed a training aircraft which was sat on the runway before returning to prepare for the next day's raids. On 20 August, the same bomber returned to Kano and this time successfully damaged a pair of MiG-17 jets. During September the newly organised Nigerian Air Force's jet strike force began to hit back at the Biafran Air Force. The Jet Provosts and MiG-17s targeted the airfields being used by the US bombers and it became difficult to keep any of them flying. At about the same

The Swedish Count Carl Gustaf von Rosen was the lifelong adventurer and supporter of lost causes who reformed the Biafran Air Force in 1969. He is seen in the cockpit of his Minicon "light sporting aircraft" which formed the new strike force of the Air Force. This civilian aircraft was converted into low-flying light-striker, through addition of two pods for unguided rockets. Flying at slow speeds they flew in at tree top level, they would fire their rockets and then fly away before the enemy could return fire. They targeted oil installations and military targets with great success throughout 1969 destroying several Nigerian jet fighters and bombers. (Private Collection)

time the Biafran Air Force commander was fatally injured in ground fighting. He was replaced by Major Godwin Ezeilo who brought a new momentum to the Biafran air campaign. He ordered that the bombing raids carried out by the RB-26P and two B-25s should be increased to try to assist the struggling Biafran ground forces. Up to three sorties a day were carried out by the exhausted handful of crew against the Federal forces at the port of Calabar. In late November it was reported that Soviet and Czech jets had arrived at the airfield at Calabar. These were Soviet MiG-17 fighter-bombers and Czech L-29 armed trainers which almost immediately destroyed the fragile Biafran air superiority. In a last gasp effort to counter this new threat the Biafrans decided to try and hit the jets on the ground. What was to prove to be the last raid of the veteran bombers took place on 2 December and involved a B-25 flown by Friedrich Herz and the RB-26P flown by Captain Durang. Herz's co-pilot was Major Ezeilo – the Air Force's commander. Their target was Nigerian troops who had recently landed at the port of Calabar and they did cause a number of casualties. When the two planes returned to their base, they were both damaged on landing and were unable to fly again. With the loss of the last of the US-made bombers the Biafrans were now basically without any combat aircraft and from now on the Nigerian MiGs were to have total air superiority.

The 'Phantom' Air Force 1968

Before the dawn of 1968, the Biafran Air Force had basically ceased to exist and all its aircraft had either been destroyed in bombing raids or captured by advancing Federal troops. In the early months of the year Colonel Ojukwu had appealed to the public for funds to buy at least six new aircraft. As all Biafrans, regardless of their wealth, were now suffering from heavy Nigerian air raids the fund had reached a level that meant at least three aircraft could be purchased. As Ojukwu's agents tried to find suitable planes to build a new air force with, the public began to doubt their leader's intentions. In early March, Biafra's phantom Air Force lost its leader when Colonel Louis Chude Sokei was killed in a car crash as he travelled to Onitsha. It took until the winter for Biafran agents to buy six ex-RAF Provost prop driven T-1 basic trainers and it was hoped that these could be converted into light strike aircraft. Although the aircraft were purchased they never got further than the British Isles where they were stored until they could be flown into Biafra. They ended up parked at a British airfield for months and the Provosts were supposed to have been scrapped by the agents involved. Instead they found their way to Rhodesia where they flew for a number of years for the embattled state. As the MiG-17s began to dominate the skies above Biafra more efforts were made to try and acquire similar aircraft to challenge them. This was to prove an extremely frustrating exercise for the Biafrans, but they were to persist with their efforts until the end of the war. In May 1968, the Biafran agents were successful in buying a pair of ex-Austrian Air Force Fouga Magisters. A single Magister used by the Katangan Air Force in the early 1960s had made a major difference to their efforts and the Biafrans had high hopes for the two they had acquired. Instead of flying the jets into Biafra they had to be flown in two pieces from Austria to be assembled closer to the rebel state. Their fuselages were flown into the West African island of Sao Tome while their wings were stored at an airfield in Portuguese Guinea. Both aircraft remained grounded throughout the war and proved to be another waste of money for the Biafrans. In another attempt to add jets to their inventory, the Biafrans managed to find four Second World War era Meteor jets from disparate sources. Two of the Meteors got as far as the Biafran Air Force's base in Europe at Faro in Portugal. There they were fitted with guns but unfortunately for the Biafran war effort they never got any further and stayed in Portugal until 1970. One successful addition to the Biafrans' air power was the gift of two DC-3 transport planes from Zambia in August 1968. Officially these aircraft were to be used to transport food from one part of Biafra to another. It appears however, that they were instead used to move arms from Uli air strip to units around the enclave. An interesting but abortive scheme involved the purchase of another pair of DC-3s from West Germany in September 1968. The transport aircraft were to be converted for ground attack duties with 9mm guns mounted in their doors, modelled on the AC-47 'Spooky' being used in Vietnam at the time armed with the rotating mini-guns and flown in circles above their target. Unfortunately for the Biafrans the scheme never came to pass, and the two were yet another waste of their scarce foreign currency.

Biafra's Aerial Lifeline

Once the naval blockade had been properly enforced by the Nigerian Navy and Army, Biafra relied almost entirely on receiving any aid from the air. During the first year of the war, before the scale of starvation in the country had been discovered, Port Harcourt airport was mainly used as a military base. When Port Harcourt fell to the Nigerians in May 1968 the Biafrans lost their major airport there. In response they set up an improvised air strip at Uli which was in fact just a cleared long straight section of tarmac road. It was situated on the main Owerri-Ihuala road which had been widened to create a 25-metre wide and 2,600-metre long landing strip. The ingenuity of Uli was that when the 'runway' was damaged by bombs another section of widened straight road close by could be opened up. Repair gangs could then repair the damaged section and the mobile control tower and landing lights could be simply switched back to the original runway. When transport planes flew in, the landing lights would be switched on for a few seconds so as not to alert any lurking Nigerian bombers to the strip's location. The large cargo planes that flew into the air strip were piloted by some of the most skilled pilots in the world. Although some aircraft did crash during the two years, the skill of the experienced pilots kept losses down to a minimum. Two other airstrips at Ugu and Agwu were also used, but Uli, code-named 'Airstrip Annabelle' was to remain the main airstrip until the end of the war. It had been designated as the only air strip which could receive food and other aid from agencies like Joint Church Aid, Save the Children and the International Red Cross. The fact that Uli was also being used to fly in arms to the Biafrans was a constant source of 'heated' debate between the Nigerians and the aid agencies. With no land or sea supply routes being agreed by the Nigerians, Uli was to remain the only way to get in or out of Biafra. It was generally agreed that Uli was the busiest airport in West Africa but was hard to see as it was surrounded by bush. Its military and civilian staff spent the day resting in camouflaged bunkers and waited for the night-time flights to begin. After the palm leaves camouflaging the runway had been removed, the 1,000 or so personnel at Uli waited for the first flights to arrive. Under cover of darkness, planes flew into the airstrip and were unloaded and flew out again with a fleet of aid agency trucks then distributing the food. At the same time arms shipments were unloaded and then whisked away to bunkers to be sorted and sent out to Biafran units. It can safely be said that Uli airstrip was the most important piece of Biafran territory and kept the war effort alive. If at any time the Nigerian Army had captured it then the war would to all intents and purposes have been over. Although the Nigerian bombers tried their best to destroy Uli, its lack of fixed facilities, such as a control tower and hangars, saved it. When Uli finally fell to the Nigerian Army on 12 January 1970 the Federal troops celebrated as if they had captured Colonel Ojukwu himself.

Resurrected Air Force of 1969

After over a year of having no air power the Biafran Air Force was reformed with the help of a life-long Swedish adventurer. The Army was continuing to resist the Federal Army but the skies were totally dominated by Nigeria's MiG-17s. With no air opposition to deal with the Nigerian fighter-bombers strafed any Biafran vehicle that moved. Nigerian Air Force aircraft were also impeding the supply flights which brought in arms for the Biafran Army. The saviour of the Biafran Air Force was 60-year-old Swedish nobleman Count Carl Gustav von Rosen, who had been flying a DC-7 supply plane into Uli Airfield. He had a history of supporting 'lost' causes, having flown for the Ethiopians during their war with Italy in 1935 – 36.

In the egalitarian atmosphere that existed in the Minicon Squadron one of the Swedish pilots Martin Lang carries his own rockets to his plane. It is perhaps surprising that the Swedes who flew the strike aircraft alongside Count von Rosen did so purely for the cause. Many admired the fight being put up by the Biafrans and were willing to risk their lives to support it. (Author's Collection)

In 1939 he flew for the Finns during their one-sided war against the Soviet Union and now sympathised with the Biafran cause. The Count formulated a plan to build an air arm which could combat the Nigerian Air Force using easily maintained light aircraft. It was hoped that this small-scale air force could disrupt the Nigerian war effort sufficiently enough to force them to sit at the peace table with the rebels. His plan which he discussed with Ojukwu and his high ranking officers was for the purchase of a fleet of modern trainer aircraft which could be converted to perform ground attack missions. Once the plan was approved Count von Rosen moved quickly to purchase five Swedish Malmo MFI-9B Mili-trainers for £541,477, supposedly to fly food and medicines to bush landing strips. In reality they were to be converted into combat aircraft by the installation of underwing rocket launchers and long-range fuel tanks. The disassembled aircraft arrived in neighbouring Gabon on 19 May 1969, where they were rebuilt and the rockets fitted. They were flown into Biafra a few days later by two Swedish and two Biafran pilots, along with von Rosen himself. One of the Biafran pilots was the Air Force commander Augustus Opke, who wanted to take an active role in the war instead of sitting behind a desk. Ground crew painted the Mili-trainers, which were commonly called Minicons in the press, with camouflage on the upper wings and body and light blue underneath. They then fitted them with French rocket launchers which could accommodate six Matra rockets under each wing. The name Minicon was said to have originated from the words 'Miniature Counter Insurgency Aircraft'.

A Portuguese pilot, Gil Pinto de Sousa flying for the Biafrans stands next to his crashed Harvard T-6G surrounded by armed Nigerian police in 1969. He had been flying his US made trainer to Biafra when its engine malfunctioned and he bailed out over Nigerian territory. After being captured he was to spend almost five years in a Nigerian jail without facing trial for his mercenary activity. (Africa Press)

Minicon Raids

The first raid of four Minicons was launched on 22 May. Led by von Rosen, it targeted the airfield outside Port Harcourt, where two MiG-17s and two Il-28 light bombers were destroyed on the ground. Two days later a second raid was launched against another military airfield, this time at Benin in the Mid-Western State where one MiG-17F and an IL-28 were damaged. A third raid on the 27th against occupied Enugu saw another two fighter-bombers and two light-bombers hit, as well as a DH Heron light transport. Next day another raid was launched on Port Harcourt but this time the targets were oil facilities and the refinery. The raids made the unit's pilots into national heroes and their 'Biafra Baby' planes became legends amongst the embattled Biafran population. Amongst the Nigerian planes destroyed in the raids was the IL-28 known as 'Intruder' which had been based at Benin Airfield as part of the so-called 'Genocide Squadron'. This aircraft, which flew at night over Biafra, had caused panic amongst the relief agency pilots: underway at an altitude above 10,000ft, it was well outside the range of any anti-aircraft weapons in the Biafran arsenal, and its destruction was cause for much celebration on the rebel side. The exploits of the Minicons may have given the population a great fillip but they did not impress some of the people who had given to Ojukwu's aircraft fund in 1968. They questioned whether these light planes had cost as much as the jet fighters and bombers that their leader had promised when he launched the campaign.

During the seven months that the Minicons were operational their chosen targets were changed on several occasions. During the first phase, the Minicons concentrated on Nigerian Air Force targets with reports of a number of MiG-17s and IL-28s being damaged. A second phase saw the oil industry hit with the Nigerian economy targeted with some success. In the third phase the planes hit concentrations of Nigerian troops as they tried to take the pressure off their beleaguered ground forces. August saw the welcome arrival of four new Minicons although a couple may have stayed in Gabon where they were used for training. In October, the Minicons were divided into two Squadrons, the 45th and 47th with between two to three aircraft available for combat at any time. At the same time the planes began to concentrate most of their attacks on the Nigerian oil industry. Throughout the second half of the month these raids intensified as the Biafran Air Force tried to harm the Nigerian economy and war effort. Attacks included one on a Dutch oil tanker which left two holes in the side of the vessel. By the end of October, the Minicon raids had effectively stopped the oil industry in the Mid-West region. They had attacked the Shell-BP terminal at Forcados which reduced the production of oil severely, causing economic problems for the Nigerian government. The Air Force now received reinforcements on 2 November in the form of three

Air Crews in 1969

When the Biafran Air Force was reformed in 1969, the fleet of MFI-9Bs – or Minicons – were initially flown almost exclusively by Swedish 'volunteers.' The Swedish pilots were Count Von Rosen himself; who was given the rank of wing commander, Gunner Haglund; now flight-lieutenant, and Martin Lang; who was created a captain. With the Swedish pilots came two ground crew; Bengt Weithz a mechanic and Sigvard Torsten Nilsson, a 58-year-old who was put in charge of ground operations. Four Portuguese pilots Gil Pinto de Sousa, Artur Alves Perieira, Jose Eduardo Peralta and Armando Cro Bras were also contracted to fly the Harvard T-6Gs which arrived later. They had all served in the Portuguese Air Force and were now in the reserves and agreed to fly for up to $3,000 per month. Cro Bras left the other three before they got to Biafra and was followed by Peralta who had at least flown his plane into the embattled enclave. The remaining pair were joined by another Portuguese, Jose da Cunha Pignatelli, to fly the only two T-6Gs that arrived at Uli. Two Portuguese ground crew also became part of the group to service the pair of T-6Gs. Eventually joining the Portuguese was the German Herz who had decided to return to Biafra and flew one of the T-6Gs. The Swedes were supported by a group of Biafran pilots made up of the two helicopter pilots, Tony Alaribe and Godwin Ezeilo – the Air Force commander. Other Biafran MFI-9B pilots were Ibi Brown, Alex Agbafuna, Augustus Opke, Willy Murray-Bruce, Johnny Chuco and Flight Lieutenant Larry Obiechi. By July 1969, the Swedes had returned home and for the last months of the war it was left to the Biafrans and Frederich Herz to fly until the end of the fighting. The Biafrans, with the help of Count von Rosen, set up training schemes for their pilots in late August and September in Gabon. All the Biafran pilots were sent on this training course and by the end of September there were 9 Biafran pilots and Herz available to fly the Minicons.

One of the two Harvard AT-6s which arrived in Biafra in late 1969 and flew missions alongside the Minicons that had been active there for several months. According to eyewitnesses who were on the receiving end of attacks by the AT-6s their pilots flew with great expertise. Keeping planes like this in the air was always a problem for the handful of mechanics and ground crews. (Author's Collection)

US Harvard Texan T-6G trainers dating back to the Second World War. One was piloted by Fred Herz, the German pilot who had briefly flown one of the B-25s on bombing raids two years before. On 9 November the Minicons suffered their first aerial loss when one was shot down by a MiG-17F. On 10 November, two T-6Gs went on their first raid against Port Harcourt Airport and shot up a number of MiG-17Fs on the runway and the two pilots claimed to have destroyed a total of three MiGs in what was described as a 'highly professional attack.' On the same day a combined force of one T-6G and three Minicons attacked the oil company airstrip at Escarvos. They damaged two military aircraft that were operating from the airstrip, a Dornier DO-27 trainer and a DC-3 transport. Four days later, a combined force of the two recently arrived AT-6s and three Minicons attacked Port Harcourt. Throughout November, and into December, the Minicon raids continued but attacks were now switched to concentrations of Nigerian troops. One of the T-6Gs was also moved closer to the front to try and counter the increasing Nigerian attacks. One such Minicon raid was reportedly against the newly arrived 122mm Soviet field guns which threatened to shut down Uli airfield. In late November the Minicons were still launching regular three-aircraft raids against any suitable Nigerian targets. On 28 November, the Biafran Air Force suffered a blow when two Minicons were destroyed on the ground by MiG-17s. Luckily their pilots, who had just returned from a mission, were able to take cover as the jets attacked. Early December saw the T-6G fleet reduced to one, not by the loss of an aircraft, but by the desertion of one of the two pilots. By late December 1969 the chronic shortage of aviation fuel meant that the Biafran Air Force was virtually finished. Morale amongst its pilots had plummeted and all of the Swedes, Portuguese and other pilots had left Biafra. Although the head of the Air Force was still looking for foreign pilots to fly the remaining aircraft, he failed to find any. Some newly trained Biafran pilots did arrive from their training school in Gabon but the general morale of the Minicon crews was very low. Any raids by the Minicons were now usually single aircraft affairs which were launched at the request of desperate Army commanders.

A Minicon was lost on 4 January when it was shot down with the loss of Flight-Lieutenant Ibi Brown. After Brown's death the Biafran Air Force now consisted of a single Minicon and a T-6G. On 8 January, Air Force commander General Ezeilo reported to the remaining pilots that Ojukwu was leaving the country and he was followed by the last Portuguese pilot, Pereira. When the Biafrans surrendered on 12 January 1970 all the remaining Minicons were captured on the ground. The last Biafran aircraft to survive in a flyable condition was an Alouette II helicopter which was flown out of the doomed country on 2 January 1970 in the cargo hold of one of the last cargo aircraft to leave the territory – but it was never flown again. The Biafran Air Force thus ceased to exist.

Chapter 7
Biafran Military Equipment and Gear

The impression that all Biafran soldiers in 1967-1970 were dressed in rags is a misconception. Although many ordinary soldiers did wear clothes with patches and holes, others managed to maintain a reasonable level of uniformity. At the start of the war the small regular army was universally dressed in a smart light khaki uniform worn with black boots and a distinctive field cap. One journalist who was in Biafra in 1967 says that most of the rebel troops were wearing uniforms which were 'pressed and they had shined their boots.'[1] Another eyewitness who saw troops on the Northern Front in mid-June commented that a well as having shiny boots, the Biafran soldiers were 'surprisingly smart, with battle packs and spanking new sub-machineguns.'[2] It was relatively easy for the Biafrans to kit out a few hundred or thousand men with uniforms and equipment. When the Biafran Army was expanding as the fighting got properly underway this was not so easy. By the summer of 1967 the shortage of boots, socks, blankets and webbing become chronic. The only real equipment that was in use with the Biafrans were the pouches and belts which arrived with the arms of Czech origin in 1966 – 67.

As the war dragged on and the number of troops in the army increased from a few thousand to about 40,000, uniforms became scarcer. As with the Federal Army, any combination of jungle green, khaki drill and camouflage uniforms were utilised by the Biafrans. In many cases just one or two items of military clothing were worn along with civilian clothing, and ordinary shirts were simply adapted by the addition of Biafran Sun patches on the shoulders. In the early days of the war when cloth was available it was dyed into either jungle green or various camouflage patterns before being made into uniforms by local tailors. Desperate measures were often taken to try and clothe the Biafran troops with at one time grey 'baft' cloth taken from warehouses dyed green and made into uniforms. The uniforms only lasted two weeks before falling apart because of the total unsuitability of the cloth used. Several textile mills and workshops were converted to produce jungle green and French-style camouflage shirts and trousers. Cloth, like everything else in Biafra, was in short supply and some uniforms were made from cast off 'salt bags' which tore easily and meant that the soldiers were soon wearing rags again. Local commanders had to often take matters into their own hands, with Colonel Rolf Steiner of the 4th Commando Brigade being a prime example. He kitted his whole unit out by buying a consignment of white cloth from a Greek trader. He had it dyed jungle green and then tailored by a few local 'master' tailors with 50 assistants with sewing machines to fit the men individually. He then acquired enough footwear for his men by doing a favour for a German who owned a shoe factory, for which the price was 2,000 pairs of boots. The standard of uniform worn by Biafran soldiers was often a matter of pure luck, with units closest to the supply depots getting the lion's share. Even if a Biafran soldier was lucky enough to be issued with a uniform when he joined the army, he was unlikely to receive replacements as his wore out. There were two issues of uniform in 1969 in the southern sector of the war but these were inadequate and didn't go around. Throughout the whole of 1969 there were no new boots issued, with the result that many had to go barefoot. In the same year, in the southern sector of the war there were two issues of uniforms but there were not enough to clothe all the troops that needed them.

Headgear

It appears that the only model of helmet in widespread use with the Biafrans was the US M1 model which were captured in some numbers from the Nigerians. Helmets were always in short supply with some units reported to have just one for every 50 men. It was usually easy to see which soldier was the senior in any Biafran unit as he often had a steel helmet and an automatic rifle. The helmets were often decorated with various insignia and mottos painted on them by their owners. Writing a phrase or motto on the helmet had become popular during the Vietnam War and was mimicked by both sides in the civil war. They often had patriotic mottos on them, such as 'Biafra Must Win' or some other similar proclamation. Others had personal phrases; some seen decorating helmets included 'Bob Go Slow!' and 'Jasper Black Tiger of the Day'. Two other types of protective headgear were not particularly useful; these were the plastic liner for the M1 and a helmet made from tinplate. The hard-plastic liners were worn as substitute helmets but of course had no protective qualities. A large number of the homemade helmets were made from sheet metal and later from discarded baby milk tins sent by aid agencies. These were cut into patterns which had been sized by using cardboard mock ups and then pressed over a head shaped cast. These distinctive looking helmets were then smoothed and shaped into something resembling an oil-worker's hard hat from the 1960s. From photographic evidence it appears that they were in widespread use, but their protective qualities were doubtful. Other headgear included the locally produced field cap which became the archetypal type during the war. Berets in various colours were also worn with some colours like red and green being worn mainly by the Commando Brigade. Other popular soft headgear included the daisy cup style jungle hat and a wide variety of civilian caps.

Footwear

Like all other uniform items, the Biafrans were desperately short of all kinds of footwear during the war. Footwear was made up of various types of combat boots captured from the Federal Army or imported and they also wore rubber Wellington boots. Combat boots were available on the army surplus market and usually arrived in unorganised batches. Soldiers had to search for matching pairs from piles, with one photograph from the war showing a small mountain of mixed up boots ready to be fought over by desperate troops. Many Biafran soldiers were forced to go barefoot or wear any civilian shoes that they could get their hands on. Some would have worn the shoes that they were wearing when they volunteered or were conscripted. These included totally unsuitable fashion shoes, like 'winkle pickers' and those donated by charities to be worn by civilians. In reality, most African men and boys did not have a spare pair of boots that were suitable for wearing in a war situation. Homemade shoes were made from any available material, including tarpaulin or goatskin for the uppers and bits of car tyres for the soles. The shortage of footwear meant that throughout the whole of 1969 no new boots were issued to the army at all. Whatever the source of footwear it was estimated that 50 percent of Biafran troops went barefoot at one time or another during the war. The lack of shoes or boots meant that soldiers often stood in flooded trenches barefooted which led to large numbers getting pneumonia. Journalists were often shocked to see the barefooted Biafrans on patrol with one commenting: "even the Viet Cong don't go barefoot."[3] The Nigerians, cruelly taking advantage of their foes' situation, began to sow the area around their positions with broken glass. When boots or shoes were delivered to units they often arrived mixed up and it was up to the soldiers to sort out a pair that might fit them.

Captured Uniforms

Throughout the war the Biafran Army relied heavily on uniforms captured from the Nigerian Army. At the start of the war the Biafrans were able to capture several large caches of Nigerian uniforms including one load of 2,000 uniforms. As the war progressed the Biafrans had to rely on capturing smaller quantities of uniforms in ambushes. In fact, most captured uniform items were pulled off captive Nigerians or taken from the bodies of dead Federal troops. In many actions the obsession of the Biafrans before going on an operation was to capture arms, equipment and uniforms. When they captured uniforms they easily adapted them by stripping the Federal insignia and adding the rising sun arm patch. Journalists were sometimes shocked at the behaviour of some Biafran troops whooping with joy as they stripped the bloody uniforms from dead Nigerians. The reality was that since time began poorly clothed armies had taken uniform items from their enemy when they could. Clever Nigerian officers learned to exploit the desperation of the Biafrans by planting uniforms in pre-targeted zones. As the Biafrans gathered their prizes together the Nigerians would drop mortar bombs on them.

Officers' Uniforms

When the war began, most pre-war Biafran officers wore their old Federal Army uniforms with Nigerian insignia and ranks removed. Most officers had two issued uniforms and were encouraged to hand their spare uniforms to brother officers. In practice, most officers were loath to hand their uniforms over as they did not know when they might receive replacements. Even the officers who kept their pre-1967 uniforms found that they began to wear out due to their constant use. Khaki drill does seem to have been popular with the officers in the early period of the war but by 1969 it would have worn out. In the last year of the war many officers were issued with new uniform jackets and trousers made from 'duck hunter' camouflage material. These uniforms were worn with surviving peaked caps or with newly made caps of the Fidel style. Most officers had a gold metal badge on the front of their field caps which was in the design of an eagle atop an elephant's tusk with the word Biafra written across it. Under the tusk were entwined metal horseshoe shapes which represented the old currency of the region. Colonel Achuzia, the extrovert Biafran commander, for some reason had painted the eagle and tusk on his cap badge in red. On the officers' peaked cap most officers had a cloth badge with the Biafran coat of arms embroidered on it. Because of the lack of standard peaked caps a variety of other soft caps were worn by the Biafran officers. By the end of the war most officers were wearing similar uniforms to the rest of the army but usually a smarter 'pressed' version.

Uniforms of the Commando Brigade

The 4th Commando Brigade wore two types of uniform; a plain green pattern and a spotted camouflage pattern. In addition to the uniforms obtained by Steiner as detailed above, by the middle of 1968 most commandos were wearing the 'duck hunter' camouflage with the addition of a beret and scarf. Coloured scarves were worn by the various units of the Brigade to distinguish different battalions, with yellow, red and blue being worn. Mention is made of the 'Ahoada Strike Force' under the command of the Corsican mercenary Armand Ianarelli as being the 'commandos of the red scarf'.[4] Other reports say that the 'Guards' unit under Taffy Williams wore blue scarves and the 'Abibiki Strike Force' under the Rhodesian Johnny Erasmus wore yellow scarves. Green scarves appear to have been worn by the officers and soldiers of the 4th Brigade who did not belong to a particular unit within it. The Brigade's headquarters staff and guards wore white scarves, usually with green berets, and often had the badges from their previous service pinned on them. This was a common habit amongst the mercenaries with, for instance, Steiner wearing his cap badge from the Foreign Legion paratroopers on his beret. A few of the commandos of the Ahoada Force were also seen wearing red berets in addition to their neckerchiefs. Some 4th Brigade Commandos who had steel helmets also stencilled the unit's skull and crossbones insignia on the front of them.

Army Insignia

The iconic symbol seen on most Biafran soldiers' uniforms or para-military dress was the black and yellow rising sun arm patch. These were easily produced locally and therefore the design varied slightly but was basically a yellow rising sun with alternate straight and wavy rays on a black patch. It was usually bordered in yellow and under the half rising sun was a yellow bar symbolising the land of Biafra. The patch was easy and cheap to produce and stood out on any uniform or civilian clothing. Biafran soldiers would sew it onto their tunics and shirts and were always proud to wear it as a symbol of their nationality. In addition to the sun patch some Biafran divisions and battalions did have their own distinctive insignia. The elite 'S' Brigade, later Division, had a black oblong patch with a red lightning strike running across it. Other Biafran unit badges appear to have been limited to Roman numerals signifying the battalion or division number. Soldiers of the Seventh and Fifth battalions were seen in photographs wearing patches with 'VII' and 'V' Roman numerals on them. Although the wearing of unit shoulder patches was not universal the 'XII' or 12th and 'XIII' or 13th Divisions definitely wore them. In the case of the 12th their patch was either black characters on a white background or white characters on a black background. The 13th Division appear to have worn patches with black characters on a white background only. Just to confuse things the 14th Battalion wore an Arabic '14' on their uniforms instead of the Roman numerals worn by other units. Some units appear to have worn unit patches made from red cloth with black Roman numerals stitched on them. In most cases the battalion numerals were in white on a black cloth patch but other examples were black on a white or yellow patch. Other arm insignia did exist, but the lack of a dress regulations and the poor-quality photographic evidence does not allow for identification. Biafran Military Police did wear black armbands with red 'MP' stencilled or painted on them. In addition, troops serving in a command post wore black armbands with the white letters 'CP' sewn on them.

Uniforms of the Biafran Navy and Air Force

The shortage of uniforms in the Army was not surprisingly mirrored in both the Biafran Navy and Air Force. Biafran Navy uniform regulations were basic with only dark blue fatigue trousers and light blue shirts, with shoulder boards for officers specified. Ratings were to wear dark blue berets while officers wore their peaked caps from their service in the Nigerian Navy if they had them. A parade uniform was also authorised with short sleeved white shirts and dark blue woollen trousers. In the dire situation faced by Biafra it is surprising that the Navy was given a budget of $278,000 to buy uniforms with. Royal Navy surplus tropical white uniforms would have been available to buy on the open market. The money available should have been more than sufficient to kit out the small number of crewmen in the Navy. Air Force uniforms for the handful of Biafran air and ground crew were totally flexible, with any military dress allowed. From photographic evidence it appears that jungle green shirts and flying trousers were popular and were worn with BAF shoulder boards. There was a specially designed brass metal badge which was worn on berets and side caps and on the front of ex-Nigerian Air Force peaked caps. From the photographic evidence it also appears that officers wore light khaki tunics and trousers with cloth belt, white shirt and black tie with a blue grey peaked cap. Flying helmets were not universally worn and when they were, they came from various surplus suppliers. The Swedish crews of the Minicon aircraft seem to have worn civilian clothing with items of flying gear brought from their homeland.

Bibliography

Please note that whilst every effort has been made to compile full bibliographic information, on occasion some details (particularly the place of publication) are not recorded.

Abbott, P., *Unknown Armies: Biafra* (unpublished manuscript, 1999).

Abubakar, Major A. A., *The Nigerian Civil War Causes, Strategies and Lessons Learnt* (Quantico: US Marine Corps Command and Staff College, 1992).

Achiebe, C., *There Was a Country* (New York: Penguin Press, 2012; ISBN-10-978-0-313-32384-3).

Achuzia, J., *Requiem Biafra* (Enugu: Fourth Dimension Publishers, 1986; ISBN-10-9789781562563).

Aguolu, C. C., *Nigerian Civil War 1967-1970 An Annotated Bibliography*(Boston: G K Hall, 1973).

Akpan, N. U., *The Struggle for Secession 1966-1970* (London: Frank Cass & Company Ltd, 1971; ISBN-0-7146-2949-9)

Alade, R. B., *The Broken Bridge: Reflections and Experiences of a Medical Doctor during the Nigerian Civil War* (The Caxton Press, West Africa, 1975).

Amadi, E., *Sunset in Biafra: A Civil War Diary* (Heinemann Educational, 1973; ISBN-10-9780435901400).

Aneke, Dr L. N., *The Untold Story of the Nigeria-Biafra War* (New York: Triumph Publishing, 2007; ISBN-10-1890430498).

Baxter, P., *Biafra: The Nigerian Civil War 1967-1970* (Solihull: Helion & Co., 2014; ISBN: 978-1-909982-36-9)

Brogan, P. & Zarca, A., *Deadly Business: The Story of Sam Cummings, the World's Greatest Arms Dealer* (London: Michael Joseph Ltd., 1984; ISBN 978-0-7181-24154).

Buhler, J., *Tuez-Les Tous! Guerre de Secession au Biafra* (Paris: Editions Flammarion, 1968; ASIN: B0014XYVPW).

Burrowes, J., *Frontline Report, A Journalists Notebook* (Edinburgh: Mainstream Publishing, 1982; ISBN-0-906391-27-X).

Cervenka, Z., *A History of the Nigerian Civil War 1967-1970* (Frankfurt am Mein: Alfred Metzner Verlag, 1971).

Collis, R., *Nigeria in Conflict* (London: Secker & Warburg, 1970; ISBN 436-10560-8).

Debre, F., *Biafra An II* (Editions Julliard, 1968).

Draper, M. I., *Shadows: Airlift and Airwar in Biafra and Nigeria 1967-1970* (Aldershot: Hikoki Publications, 1999; ISBN 9781902109633).

Dudley, B. J. *Instability and Political Order: Politics and Crisis in Nigeria* (Ibadan: Ibadan University Press, 1973; ISBN 9789781210464).

Effiong, P., *Nigeria & Biafra: My Story* (African Tree Press, 2007; ISBN 978-1-59232-013-9).

Ebbe, I., *Broken Back Axle: Unspeakable Events in Biafra* (Bloomington: Xlibris Corporation, 2010; ISBN 978-1-4535-7360-0).

Falola, T. & Ezekwemi, O., *Writing the Nigeria-Biafra War* (Martlesham: Boydell & Brewer, 2016; ISBN -9781847011442).

Forsyth, F., *The Biafra Story* (London: Penguin, 1969; ISBN 978-0-7278-0978-4).

Forsyth, F., *Emeka* (New Delhi: Spectrum Books, 1982; ISBN 9789782462091).

Forsyth, F., *The Outsider* (New York: G.P Putnam's & Sons, 2015; ISBN 978-0-399-17607-4).

Gould, M. *The Biafran War: The Struggle for Modern Nigeria* (London: Tauris & Co, 2012; ISBN 978-1-78076-463-4).

Hilton, Br., *Highly Irregular* (New York: The Macmillan Company, 1969).

Jowett, P., *The Nigerian-Biafran War 1967-70 (Modern African Wars No.5)* (Oxford: Osprey Publishing Ltd., Modern African Wars No.5; ISBN 978-1-4728-1609-2).

Kirk-Greene, A. *Crisis and Conflict* (New York: Oxford University Press, 1975; ISBN 9780192156419).

Lantier, J., *Le Temps des Mercenaries: Faut-il les condamner?* (Verviers Gérard et Cie., coll Bibliothèque Marabout, No. 338, 1969).

Legum, C. & Drysdale, J., *Africa Contemporary Record 1968-1969* (Africana Research Ltd., 1969).

Luckham, R., *The Nigerian Military: A Sociological Analysis of Authority and Revolt 1960-67* (New York: Cambridge University Press, 1971; ISBN 978-0521098823).

Madiebo, A. A., *The Nigerian Revolution and the Biafran War* (Enugu: Fourth Dimension Publishers, 1980; ISBN-978-156-1173).

McCullin, D., *Unreasonable Behaviour: An Autobiography by Don McCullin* (London: Jonathan Cape Ltd., 1990; ISBN-0099437767).

Miners. N. J., *The Nigerian Army 1956-1966* (London: Methuen, 1971; ISBN 978-0416658606).

Mockler, A. *The New Mercenaries* (Saint Paul: Paragon House, 1985; ISBN 978-0913729724).

Mok, M., *Biafra Journal* (New York: Time Life Books, 1969; ISBN BWB14287465).

Nwankwo, A. A. & Ifejika, S. U. *The Making of a Nation: Biafra, My People Suffer* (London: C Hurst & Company, 1969; ISBN 9780900966125).

Niven, Sir R. *The War of Nigerian Unity* (Totowa: Evans Brothers, Ltd. 1970).

Njoku, H.M., *A Tragedy Without Heroes: The Nigeria-Biafra War* (Enugu: Fourth Dimension Publishers, 1987; ISBN-978-156-279-X).

Nowamagbe, A. O. MD MPH FACC, *The Mid-West Invasion of 1967: Lessons for Today's Geopolitics* (Text of Keynote speech, South Carolina, 1998).

Nwankwo, A. A., *Nigeria: The Challenge of Biafra* (Enugu: Fourth Dimension Publishers, 1972; ISBN 978-156-065-7).

Nzimiro, Ikenna – *Nigerian Civil War – A Study in Class History* (Enugu: Frontline Publishing Ltd 1982; ISBN 978-156-054-1).

Obasanjo, Olusegun – *Nzeogwu* (Ibadan: Spectrum Books Ltd, 1987; ISBN 978-029-134-2).

Odu. P.J., *The Future That Vanished: A Biafra Story* (Xlibris Corporation, 2009; ISBN 978-1-4415-3972-4).

Ogbudinkpa, R. N., *The Economics of the Nigerian Civil War and its Prospects for National Development* (Enugu: Fourth Dimension Publishers, 1985; ISBN 978-156-222-6).

Okpaku, J., (editor), *Nigeria: Dilemma of Nationhood* (New York: The Third Press, 1972; ISBN 9780893881177).

Oyewole, F., *Reluctant Rebel* (London: Rex Collings, 1975; ISBN 9780901720665).

Oyinbo, J., *Nigeria: Crisis and Beyond* (London: Charles Knight & Co. Ltd., 1971; ISBN 85314-072-3).

Samueli, M. A. (editor), *The Nigeria-Biafra Conflict* (Georgetown: The Center for Strategy and International Studies, Georgetown University, 1969).

Schwab, P. (editor), *Biafra* (New York: Facts on File Inc., 1971; ISBN 0-87196-192-X).

Schwarz, W., *Nigeria* (New York: Pall Mall Press, 1968; ISBN 9780269161582).

Spencer, D., 'Armoured Combat of the Nigerian Civil War, 1967-1970', *Museum Ordnance: The Magazine for the US Army Ordinance Museum*, Volume 6, No.1, January 1996.

Stafford, Major M. R., *Quick Kill in Slow Motion: The Nigerian Civil War* (Quantico: US Marine Corps Command and Staff College, 1984).

Steiner, R. *The Last Adventurer: From Biafra to the Sudan* (Sao Paulo: Opera Mundi, 1976; ISBN 978-0-297-77363-1).

Stremlau, J. J., *The International Politics of the Nigerian Civil War, 1967-1970* (Princeton: Princeton University Press, 1977; ISBN 0-691-07857-5).

St. Jorre, J. de, *The Brothers War: Biafra & Nigeria* (London: Hodder & Stoughton, 1973; ISBN 0-340-12640-X).

Thayer, G., *The War Business* (London: Simon & Schuster, 1969; ISBN 978-0671201913).

Tickler, Peter, *The Modern Mercenary* (Wellingborough: Patrick Stephens Ltd., 1987; ISBN 0850598125).

Venter, A. J., *Africa at War* (Old Greenwich: Devin Adair Co., 1974; ISBN 73-88037).

Venter, A. J., *Biafra's War 1967-1970: A Tribal Conflict in Nigeria that left a Million Dead* (Solihull: Helion & Co, 2015; ISBN 978-1-910294-69-7).

Venter, A. J. *Biafra Genocide, Nigeria: Bloodletting and Mass Starvation 1967-1970* (Barnsley: Pen & Sword, 2018; ISBN-152672913X).

Wolf, J. & Brovelli, C., *La Guerre des Rapaces* (Paris: Editions Albin Michel, 1969; ASIN B07NZJC88).

Worthington, P., *Looking For Trouble* (Toronto: Key Porter Books, 1984; ISBN 0-919493-80-7).

Zumbach, J., *On Wings of War: My Life as a Pilot Adventurer* (New York: Harper Collins, 1975; ISBN 9780233966236).

Periodicals

'Nigeria at War', *Africa Report*, February 1968.

'Biafran Babies… The Five Aircraft Air Force', *Air Enthusiast*, Volume 38, January-April 1989.

'Biafra's Air Force', *Aircraft Illustrated*, November 1969.

The Bulletin (26 August 1967; 15 June 1968; 6 July 1968; 20 July 1968; 10 August 1968; 17 August 1968; 5 October 1968; 7 December 1968).

'Current Notes On International Affairs', Department of External Affairs, Canberra, Australia (December 1967; August 1968; December 1968; April 1969; May 1969; January 1970).

Daily Express (10 December 1969).

Daily Telegraph Magazine, 'Legacy of a War: Special Report from Biafra', 23 August 1968.

'My Summer Vacation in Biafra', *Harper's Magazine*, November 1969.

Le Nouvel Observateur (19 January 1968; 8 September 1968).

Life Magazine (12 July 1968; 23 August 1968; 23 January 1970; 30 January 1970).

'Biafra', *Look Magazine*- Biafra, 1 April 1968.

Jowett, P, 'War on a Shoestring', *Military Illustrated*, Issue 108, 1997.

Newsweek, 'Biafra at the Brink' (26 June 1967); 'Nigeria: Bloodbath on the River' (10 June 1968); 'Nigeria, the War grinds on' & 'Running the Biafran Gauntlet – for Money' (12 August 1968); 'For Biafra Time is Running Out' (19 August 1968); 'Nigeria's Deadly Stalemate' (16 December 1968); 'What to do with Biafra' (21 December 1968); 'The Resurrection of Biafra' (24 March 1969); 'Nigeria Closing the Ring on Biafra' (28 April 1969); 'Nigeria Tightens the Noose on Biafra' (14 July 1969).

Readers Digest, 'Biafra: A Nation is Dying', March 1969; 'Time for Action on Biafra', May 1969.

The Sun, 'Land of No Hope', 12 June 1968.

Sunday Telegraph, 'The Colonel Scott Report', 11 January 1970.

Sunday Times Magazine, 'Biafra: The Darkness of Africa', 9 June 1968.

Time Magazine, 'Fighting in the Mist' (28 July 1967); 'Anybody's War' (18 August 1967); 'The Little Country that won't give up' (8 December 1967); 'The Art of Resistance' (9 February 1968); 'From Hell Sector to the Conference Table' (31 May 1968); 'The Plight of the Biaffran Children' (12 July 1968); 'Agony in Biafra' (2 August 1968), 'Biafra's Agony' (23 August 1968); 'Biafra's Two Wars (30 August 1968); 'The Fall of Aba' (13 September 1968); 'Thunder Road to Umhuahia' (4 October 1968); 'The Mercenaries' (25 October 1968); 'Keeping Biafra Alive' (6 December 1968); 'Tragedy in the Villages' (7 March 1969); 'Attack on a Village' (4 April 1969); 'How to Build an Instant Air Force' (6 June 1969); 'Grim Anniversary' (4 July 1969); 'Biafra End of Rebellion (26 January 1970).

Valeurs Actuelles, 31st July 1968.

Venture Magazine, 'How Biafra Pays For the War' (March 1969); 'At The Front' (July 1969); 'Guerrilla Warfare in Biafra' (September 1969).

Notes

Introduction
1 Njoku, *A Tragedy Without Heroes.*
2 *Canberra Times*, 3 June 1967.

Chapter 1
1 The Biafran Army commander, Major-General Madeibo described Archibong as, 'one of the bravest officers I have ever met'. Archibong's luck finally ran out during the battle for Ikot-Epene, where he was killed. For details, see Madiebo, *The Nigerian Revolution and the Biafran War.*
2 Nwankwo, *Nigeria.*

Chapter 2
1 The common term of abuse used for Nigerian soldiers by the Biafrans.
2 *Venture*, July 1969.
3 Worthington, *Looking for Trouble.*
4 Effiong, *Nigeria & Biafra.*
5 *Time Magazine* 26 January 1970.
6 *Canberra Times*, 4 August 1969.
7 Achuzia, *Requiem Biafra.*
8 *NYT*, 30 September 1969.
9 Effiong, *Nigeria & Biafra.*
10 *NYT*, 25 August 1969. Notably, the tactics in question were developed from the experience of first wounding an elephant, and then rushing it, from earlier times.
11 Ibid, 6 August 1968.
12 Stafford, *Quick Kill in Slow Motion.*

Chapter 3
1 Indeed, it was reported that Watson was the man behind the development of the Ogbunigwe although this would be hotly disputed by RAP scientists who claimed to have invented it from scratch.
2 *Africa Report*, February 1968.
3 According to contemporary press-reports, only 300 troops of the 4th Brigade were confirmed as killed in this campaign: another 2,200 had been wounded, while no fewer than 4,000 were declared as missing in action.
4 *NYT*, 8 September 1968. Notably, all of the journalists that visited Steiner, his colleagues, and the 4th Commando Brigade, were impressed by their attitude. One described them, as 'not like the alcoholics, perverts, dope addicts and safe blowers' that served in the Congo… and none of the 'mercenaries…said to "kill for kicks" and who "despised the Congolese and everything "black"'.
5 *Time Magazine*, 30 August 1968.
6 Prior to this attack, the French news team interviewed two of the mercenaries. Goosens was frank in stating his main motivation was money, while Williams said he wanted to 'fight Communism.' Notably, the US$5,000 that Goosens carried on him at the time of his death (from a bullet to the stomach and another to the head) first 'went missing', but were quickly found and recovered by a furious Williams.
7 An alternative version of Neeley's death is that he might have been killed by another mercenary, under the cover of fighting.
8 *NYT*, 16 February 1970.

Chapter 4
1 Forsyth, *Emeka.*
2 *NYT*, 22 April 1968.
3 *Venture*, July 1969.
4 *Time Magazine*, 7 March 1969.
5 *Daily Telegraph*, 23 August 1968.
6 *NYT*, 22 September 1968.
7 Burrowes, *Frontline Report.*
8 McCullin, *Unreasonable Behaviour.*
9 *Time Magazine*, 23 August 1968.
10 Forsyth, *Biafra Story.*
11 Steiner, *The Last Adventurer.*
12 *NYT*, 4 December 1968.
13 It is possible that some of these were T-16 carriers (Swiss version of the Universal Carrier), about 300 of which were reportedly acquired from a Canadian arms dealer by 'East Nigerians' in 1965. However, it remains unconfirmed if any of the vehicles in question actually reached Biafra: if they did, they were almost certainly converted into so-called Red Devils.
14 Spencer, *Armoured Combat.*
15 *NYT*, 9 March 1969.
16 Ogbudinkpa, *The Economics of the Nigerian Civil War.*
17 *The Daily Express*, 10 December 1969.
18 *NYT*, 22 April 1968.
19 Ogbudinkpa, *The Economics of the Nigerian Civil War.*

Chapter 5
1 Gould, *The Biafran War.*
2 *NYT*, 18 June 1967.
3 *NYT*, 10 May 1968.
4 *Canberra Times*, October 1968.
5 *NYT*, 2 February 1969.
6 *NYT*, 2 June 1969.
7 *Time Magazine*, 4 April 1969
8 Ibid.
9 *Der Spiegel*, 17 February 1969.
10 *NYT*, 13 September 1969.
11 Marasmus is the side effect of starvation which produces a skeletal appearance of the victim and Kwashiokor is the swelling of the victim's stomach caused by lack of protein.
12 *NYT*, 16 October 1969.
13 Forsyth, *Biafra Story.*

Chapter 7
1 *NYT*, 10 June 1967.
2 *Canberra Times*, 10 July 1967.
3 *Canberra Times*, 13 March 1969.
4 Mockler, *The New Mercenaries.*

About the Author

Philip Jowett was born in Leeds, West Yorkshire, in 1961 and developed a strong interest in history from an early age. His main passion has always been military history and he has studied the subject since the 1970s. Jowett published his first military history book in 1997 and has meanwhile penned more than 30 titles, specialising in the armies of China in the first half of the 20th century, and – more recently – on Latin American conflicts. After writing a number of articles and books about the Nigerian Civil War – a conflict that deeply impressed him as a child – *The Biafran Army 1967-70* is his first instalment for Helion.